DRUM'S
RING

*Also by Richard S. Wheeler
in Large Print:*

The Buffalo Commons
Cashbox
Deuces and Ladies Wild
Dodging Red Cloud
The Final Tally
Flint's Gift
Flint's Honor
Flint's Truth
Goldfield
Incident at Fort Keogh
Montana Hitch
Rendezvous
Restitution
Sam Hook
Sierra
Where the River Runs
Winter Grass

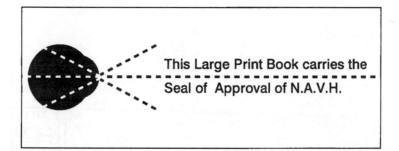

This Large Print Book carries the
Seal of Approval of N.A.V.H.

DRUM'S RING

Richard S. Wheeler

G.K. Hall & Co. • Waterville, Maine

Published in 2002 by arrangement with NAL Signet, a division of Penguin Putnam Inc.

G.K. Hall Large Print Western Series.

The text of this Large Print edition is unabridged.
Other aspects of the book may vary from the original edition.

Set in 16 pt. Plantin by Christina S. Huff.

Printed in the United States on permanent paper.

Library of Congress Cataloging-in-Publication Data

Wheeler, Richard S.
    Drum's ring / Richard S. Wheeler.
      p. cm.
   ISBN 0-7838-9640-9 (lg. print : hc : alk. paper)
   1. Women newspaper editors — Fiction. 2. Newspaper
   publishing — Fiction. 3. Kansas — Fiction. 4. Large type
   books. I. Title.
PS3573.H4345 D78 2001
  813'.54—dc21   2001053248

To my bride, Suzanne

PROLOGUE

Call me the Witness. That's what this is all about. I was christened Horatio Bates, but that's not so important. I have witnessed the stories of extraordinary people and am taking pains to set these to paper so that the whole world might celebrate lives lived with courage and honor and integrity. That's what is important.

All you need to know about me could fit into a thimble. I am a postmaster, a confirmed bachelor, an untidy man, and somewhere in my middle years; just where on the downhill slope is my private business. Delivering the United States mail may be my vocation, but it is not what galvanizes me and inspires my life.

You might wonder about a man who drifts from one frontier town to another, setting up shop wherever Uncle Sam deems the need sufficient to employ a full-time postmaster. There aren't many such burgs in the West. In most places the Post Office simply contracts with a local merchant to pop the mail into some cubbyholes in the corner of his emporium.

But I drift from town to town by choice because I like to observe frontier people. They are a breed apart, you know. Out here a man is on his own, and his inner nature determines his fate. There's little law, little order, and little charity to help a person along, so what counts on the frontier is pluck, courage, integrity, and honor.

You see, I have always been fascinated by virtue, and what it means to us all. I've witnessed amazing things: redoubtable people who refused to sell their souls, who would not cave in to evil, no matter what pressures were put on them. These are true heroes and heroines, and worthy of attention. My true vocation, then, is not delivering mail, but collecting stories about people who have been tempted by evil and refused to sell out.

Take Angie Drum, the subject of the present story. She owned a little newspaper in the cowtown of Opportunity. And she had a vision of the good commonwealth that she refused to compromise, in spite of pressures and sorrows that would break a less resolute woman. So here is her amazing story, just as I have witnessed it.

— Horatio Bates, Postmaster
Opportunity, Kansas

CHAPTER 1

Word of Bo Waggoner's suicide arrived just as Angie Drum was winding up the presswork. She had printed one side of the four-page *Opportunity Outlook* and had almost completed the other when Wim Cologne burst in with the news.

Cologne peddled fresh gossip when he could, stale gossip the rest of the time.

"Miss Angie, old Bo's done shot himself in the Stockmen's Hotel. A forty-four caliber bullet right through the left eye!"

"Bo Waggoner?"

"The most important Texan ever to come up the Chisholm, I'd say. Dead as a cheating wife. Now that's news."

Angie's bones ached. Stomping an old Hoe Washington press into printing two-hundred-seventy copies of her paper was about all she could manage without help.

She made a swift decision. "All right, thank you, Wim."

"You gonna stop the presses? Run a extry?"

"No," she replied, wearily.

"But it's the biggest story since that drunken butcher operated on his own, ah . . ."

"I'm tired. You go watch and keep me posted."

The pimpled youth burst into the unsuspecting street, not bothering to latch the doors. It didn't matter. Angie felt hot anyway.

She would finish the run. Wearily she loaded another sheet and lowered the platen. With a clank the old press imprinted pages two and three on the sheet. She lifted the sheet and loaded another. Her hands were ink stained, and her muscles protested, but she had only ten or eleven to go. A few minutes later she completed the last of these and set the papers in an orderly pile to dry overnight. In the morning, she would fold and deliver them.

She didn't want to cover a story at midnight; she wanted some well-deserved sleep after putting *The Outlook* to bed one more time. The paper had survived four years of frontier vicissitudes. She had gathered the news, hawked the ads and subscriptions, set and broke down the type, billed advertisers, and swept the shop every week for as long as she could remember.

Up until two years previous, it had really been her husband Gideon's rag, but as Paducah corn whiskey pickled him she assumed more and more of the burden. Finally, she eased him out of the paper, and he sagged onto barstools or into his one and a half rockered chair at home and guzzled until he croaked. He had died when he rocked back too far and busted his head on the woodstove.

Now she ran the paper. Her son, Martin, was part-time mayor and full-time saloonkeeper.

She had no other live children, but three dead. They were Iowa people, and she had never heard of a Hawkeye who quit.

Opportunity sulked on the left bank of the Little Arkansas River, in the epicenter of bloody Kansas; one of several cattle towns built along the steel rails of the Santa Fe Railroad, which was gradually laying rail to somewhere or other in Colorado. Ever since the war, cussing Texans had been ambushing unbranded longhorns and driving them north to markets. The railroad shipped thousands of them from Opportunity each year.

She wiped down her enemy, the press, and thought about Bo Waggoner and wondered why he had died. She would have to go find out. If the story were important enough she would do a small insert, the size of a piece of stationery, and tuck one into each copy of *The Outlook*. She dreaded that. It would keep her up all night, but she could not distribute a paper tomorrow that lacked the most important story of the summer.

She scarcely knew Bo Waggoner, but felt sorry about his death. He wasn't the usual sort of Texan, all balls and brawl. Waggoner had been quiet, thoughtful, well-spoken, but just as hard as the rest who followed the Chisholm Trail. Weak men didn't make it. Lightning, Jayhawkers, stampedes, Indians, disease, snakes, drought, bandits, or most commonly, rebellious cowboys with mean fists had ruined many a hopeful cattle drive.

She wondered how many of Bo's six sons had accompanied him this time. He had sired eight in all down there in the hills west of San Antonio, but two were in their graves. That's one thing that made Bo's drives different: there were always five or six Waggoners in the outfit.

She abraded her hands with gritty soap, knowing the futility of scrubbing the ink stains out of her fingers. Operating a press wasn't a woman's occupation, but she had done it anyway. Mostly, running a weekly paper was dull, exasperating, tedious work. But there weren't very many jobs in the world that weren't dull.

The night air felt warm and moist, and she didn't need a shawl. She collected a pencil and a wad of newsprint and headed out on the clay street. The Stockmen's Hotel rose two stories only a block away, and she wondered why she hadn't heard the shot. She usually heard all the shots in Opportunity, most of them from the cowboy dives along Lone Star Street, the wild district a block south of respectable Kansas Street, where her paper was housed.

Why had Bo Waggoner shot himself? If she found out, she would have a story worth printing that very night. If she didn't, she would have only an obituary, which could wait until the next issue.

She dragged herself over to the clapboard hotel, preferring the middle of the dirt street so that the footpads lying in wait between the frame buildings wouldn't pounce. Not that she was carrying cash. Opportunity's law enforcement was selective, something that she had complained about to Marty.

She arrived at the veranda of the odorous hotel just as the natty town marshal, Spade Ball, and the banty undertaker, Jasper Dill, were wrestling Waggoner's shrouded body out the door. Some of the Waggoner boys followed, looking pretty solemn. The marshal lowered the carcass into the bed of Dill's black-enameled Mariah and straightened up.

"What happened, Spade?" she asked.

"Waggoner blew his brains into the wall, Angie."

"Why?"

"That ain't anything a marshal can figure out, short of being a mind reader."

The three Waggoner boys stared.

She turned to them. "I'm sorry about your pa. Was something wrong?"

They seemed reluctant to talk, each glancing at the others.

"You want to come over to the paper and talk?"

"No, ma'am. We just want to git home."

"Not before you pay me for planting him," said Dill. "I'll be at the store. You come make arrangements."

"Reckon not tonight," said Joe, the older of the Waggoners.

Angie caught an undertone that troubled her.

13

"Just you three came this time?" she asked.

The boys didn't reply.

She turned to Spade. "What happened?"

The town marshal seemed reluctant to talk. "Clerk heard a shot at about eleven-ten. Went up there and found Waggoner on the bed, bullet hole in his head, his six-gun in his hand, and blood everywhere. That's all there be in it."

"You don't know any reason?"

"A man gets down, I guess."

"What possessions did he have?"

"Not much. You don't come up the trail with baggage."

"Money?"

"No . . ."

"Spade, he just came up the trail and sold a couple thousand beeves to the shippers. He had to have money."

"You just don't worry your pretty head about it, Angie. I got to write up a report."

The usual dodge. "I'm not done with you, Spade. I'll have my answers and *The Outlook*'s going to print them."

Spade smiled lazily. A woman-dismissing smile, she thought.

She had never liked him. He oozed something that she detested, but she could never put a word to it. He wasn't a strutting peacock, wasn't gaudily dressed, wasn't particularly arrogant, wasn't mean or murderous, wasn't secretive or cruel, wasn't greedy, wasn't a swine, and yet something within her told her the town marshal was all of those things. A puzzle.

Dill clambered up to his wagon seat and hawed the black dray horse. She watched it clop into the night. The marshal drifted toward the fieldstone town lockup two blocks east. The one-room jail and police office saw plenty of live bodies during the summer trail-drive season, but was mostly empty other times.

An eerie quiet settled over Kansas Street. Most lamps were out. A coy moon, silvering small clouds, threw a pale light over Opportunity. A wind off the prairies brought the pungency of grass to town.

"You men must feel pretty low," she said. "You come on down to *The Outlook*, and I'll stoke up the stove and make some java."

The Waggoners glanced nervously at one another and then agreed. There were things here she intended to probe. These silent boys weren't acting the way Texans in a cowtown acted.

They followed her wordlessly as she picked her way down the street, dodging manure. She wanted nothing more than to go to bed. A fifty-three-year-old bony woman with a little arthritis needed plenty of rest.

She led them into the clapboard false-front building. The one lamp she had left lit cast a gloomy light over the ink-stained pressroom behind her office. There weren't chairs enough for them all, so she motioned them to sit and busied herself kindling a fire and starting a pot of coffee to percolating.

15

"It'll be ready in a while. You must be feeling pretty bad. I can't get you straight, so you'd better tell me your names."

"Joe."

"Dog — actually Doug."

"Foley — named after my ma."

"You all the Waggoners that came up?"

They paused again, as if an answer would hurt.

"Well," said Joe, "Ring and Billy are in the jail."

"So's the rest of the crew," added Dog.

Angie knew she was on the brink of a story. "Your pa got paid, didn't he? For two thousand head?"

"Actually, less. But yeah, McCoy paid him," Joe said.

"Then where is the money?"

"Miz Angie, there ain't any now."

"Where did it go?"

"Ma'am, your boy's the mayor, ain't he?"

She nodded.

"Then I guess we'll not say."

CHAPTER 2

Angie retreated. Here were the Waggoner boys, full of grief, and she was badgering them for a story.

"Your pa was a good man. Thank you for answering my questions. I'm sorry about what happened," she said.

They slouched there in the wavering lamplight, big, dark, stocky men numbed with shock, pain etched in their faces. She guessed that Foley was the youngest, about fourteen. She could scarcely imagine what thoughts paraded behind their eyes because their faces were etched in granite.

"Look, just because the mayor's my son doesn't mean I like everything that's going on around here. You want some coffee? I think it's done."

"I think we'll go, ma'am," Dog said.

"Go where? You have a room?"

Joe shook his head.

No money. That was the strangest part. They would end up unrolling their blankets in the livery barn, the last refuge of broke cowboys.

"I guess we'll skip the coffee, ma'am," Joe said. The other boys seemed to take direction from him.

17

Angie didn't mind. She stood, absently lifting the pot from the cooktop of the stove.

"Do you need anything? You want to sleep in here?"

"No, ma'am."

"I guess you just want to bury your pa."

"Take him back to Texas if we can. We don't want to bury him in no Yankee Kansas cowtown that'll blow away in five years. We got a home, a *place*, where the grass grows."

"Joe, you want me to find a preacher?"

"No, we can't pay. We can't even pay that undertaker for a box."

"You have friends here?"

"Not likely. No Texians, anyway. We were ahead of most of the herds. Bo, he knew how to push."

"Your crew?"

The three glanced at one another. "We can't get 'em out."

"What are they in the pokey for?"

"Don't rightly know, ma'am," Joe said.

"Being Texians," Foley said. "That's why."

They drifted toward the double doors.

"I'm sorry. God, why did this happen?" she asked.

They filed into the night. A breeze slid through the grimy newspaper office.

"I'll say a little prayer for your pa," she yelled after them.

But they were gone. She peered into the gloomy main street of Opportunity, wondering what dark secrets lay hidden in the booming cowtown.

She said a little prayer for Bo Waggoner. She didn't know what she believed, but she had never felt that mankind walked the earth alone.

She latched the front doors, hid the day's receipts — eleven dollars and some dimes — in the wood box behind the stove, and headed for the back alley. Tomorrow she would fold and deliver the issue. Next week she would publish more of a story.

Maybe.

She hiked the three blocks to her two-room cottage. It was on the wrong side of town, not far from the sporting district. Weekly papers made no one rich. She carried a walking stick for protection, not that a few whacks with a cane would deter a drunken cowboy.

She wondered why the hell she was printing a weekly almost singlehandedly in a windy Kansas cowtown without so much as a decent restaurant. That was simple. Wherever Gideon set up a paper, she went, too. He died; she continued making the only living she knew.

But she thought she ought to sell out if she could find some itinerant printer to buy it. She couldn't even get help. She needed a printer's devil, but no kid in a wild cowtown wanted to be a printer, and most lasted less than two weeks. So she had soldiered on, not knowing what else to do.

She didn't see much of Martin, and in truth,

they had grown apart. He seemed to have plenty of money, more than his seventy-five-dollar-a-month mayor salary, but he owned the Lone Star Saloon, and that was a big draw all summer. She saw him whenever he didn't like a story or wanted the paper to hush up about something. That happened now and then. Usually she printed something anyway, just to show him who owned the paper. She loved Martin, little smiley Marty with his greased-back fuzzy hair, like his dad, but, God, he put her in a bind sometimes. The name, Opportunity, had some ironic connotations. There was a little too much opportunity in town, and people got hurt.

Like Bo Waggoner, cattleman, who had sold off a Texas trail herd and hadn't a dime to show for it.

She sank into the Morris chair, her proudest possession, and sat in the darkened room, too weary to light an oil lamp. She did that often, liking to take stock of herself and her day. She wondered what Gideon would do with a hot potato like this. Not the fumbling, whiskey-shot Gideon, but the one she married on a wild whim, the bright, journeyman printer with a philosophy for every problem and more answers than there were questions.

Gideon never belonged in sedate and proper Iowa; he belonged out among his own kind, the half-tamed, half-wild denizens of cow camps

20

and mining towns and every saloon in the West. Back there in Cedar Rapids, he had mongoosed her into marriage, scandalized her folks, and then left the black Iowa topsoil behind them. She had never regretted it, not even when Gideon had crawled into a flask and never came out.

She had learned something from him: Newspapers had to have integrity in their ironclad, honest, forthright coverage of a town. If a paper toadied to the powers that be, whether politicians in city hall or advertisers or anyone else, they were worthless. *The Outlook* wasn't worthless, and never would be so long as she ran it and the town prospered. That's what Gideon gave her, and it was her inheritance.

The next morning she folded the papers, addressed the handful that went to the post office, where Horatio Bates would see to them; and turned the rest over to her two devilish delivery boys, who would distribute the June 17 issue to subscribers and then hawk the rest on Main Street. She decided to do nothing about the Waggoner suicide for the moment; she would have a powerful story next week.

She broke down the headline type, pitching the letters into the case box, but her thoughts weren't on her work. They were rummaging the mystery of the Texan's suicide. She had so many questions that she scarcely knew where to begin, but thought she would start with the marshal.

At least he or his deputy, Eddie Farrar, would be up. She could never reach her son before noon because he kept saloon hours.

For a cowtown at the apex of the shipping season, Opportunity seemed unusually quiet. But news of Waggoner's suicide would not sit still, and she guessed that every merchant in town had heard it, along with most of the rest of town. Waggoner was one of the most important cattlemen to ship from Opportunity.

By eleven, the remains of the old paper had vanished into the type cases, and she plucked up a notebook and pencil and plunged into an airless, glowering day that promised boiler heat by mid-afternoon.

She found Farrar mucking out the cell with a mop.

"Who you got in there, Eddie?"

"No one, Miz Drum."

"How many last night?"

"A few. Spade let 'em all go."

Wordlessly she circled the desk, opened the record book, and studied the entries for the last forty-eight hours. Pretty quiet, except for seven hands from Kerrville, Texas, Flying W men.

They had been locked up without being charged. That was common enough. There was no evidence of arraignment.

"No court appearances, Eddie?"

"Nah. Spade just cools 'em down, sobers 'em up overnight, and lets 'em loose."

"That's a little informal."

"It don't clutter up the courts, Angie."

"It sure clutters up Spade's pockets, though."

Farrar laughed. The quake started in his cantilevered gut and broke upward.

"The Flying W men had some cash in their britches?"

"How should I know? Don't the trail bosses always pay their hands first off?"

"Have you seen the Waggoner boys?"

"I heard tell they're getting out of town."

She decided to find out. Maybe this morning they would open up to her.

"You tell Spade to keep better records and list fines, or I'll write about it," she said. "This is no way to enforce town ordinances."

Farrar chuckled. "You go write 'er up, Angie."

Dismissed again. That's how men treated her. The women mostly snubbed her. A woman reporter and editor was thought to be in the same league as actresses, and every respectable woman knew all about actresses. To make matters worse, unladylike utterances sometimes escaped Angie's lips. She didn't care. She liked men better anyway. She had few friends, and even those were exclusively male.

She headed into the steaming morning, uncertain about what to do next. She had found out exactly nothing. She decided to talk to Marty. Only this time she wasn't just going to talk to him, she was going to give him a little maternal jalapeña. Frontier towns were pretty relaxed, and she didn't mind that. But Spade

23

was obviously extorting money and maybe property from cowboys, and she intended to put a stop to it.

Marty had rooms above his Lone Star Saloon, accessible only from a separate side door. She hiked across the silvery rails, passed the white clapboard station, and pierced the wild side; the cowboy and cattlemen's side where saloons, variety theaters, billiard parlors, cigar stores, dance halls, and other dubious enterprises catered to the appetites of randy young bucks drovering cattle up the Chisholm Trail.

She climbed the long funereal stairs to her son's rooms and knocked on the grimy four-panel door. It wasn't noon yet, but she had questions that begged for answers.

CHAPTER 3

Marty Drum knew how to get ahead in the world. The prerequisites were a ready smile, a hand around the shoulder, a genuine interest in whoever you were with, and secrecy.

Especially secrecy. A man could not rise in politics without understanding the importance of a closed mouth.

He had won that understanding early in life when dealing with his parents, especially his mother. His father he could always cope with; his mother had been another matter. A beaming smile usually trumped her, but stealth was better. By adolescence he had become artful at dodging his mother's questions and disciplines, evading the questions with a smiling shrug or a small fib, and perfecting a certain glossy exterior obedience to her strong will.

Angie Drum had hammered the idea of good character into Marty from the moment he could understand. Perhaps it was because she was coping with a boozy and drifting husband, or perhaps it was just her own deeply rooted sense of right and wrong. Whatever the case, Marty had heard all the old bromides, such as two wrongs don't make a right. Later, he discovered that his mother's aphorisms made great political rhetoric.

Now, with Angie patrolling his parlor, having rousted him from a warm and double-occupied bed, he yawned amiably, patted Angie's stained hand, listened carefully, and said as little as possible. He wore his blue silk robe and lamb's wool slippers and thought he looked mighty fine, even if dark stubble peppered his face. How else to deal with a mother who was also the editor of the only paper in Opportunity? He never quite knew whether Angie was being a mother or reporter, but on this occasion she clearly wanted some sensitive information.

"This has gone too far," she said. "Spade's pocketing a lot of money that belongs to the city. And he's dragging those Texas cowboys into jail on any excuse. Where's the justice in that?"

"Oh, I haven't heard of it," Marty responded.

She withered him under her glare. "Don't give me that guff."

"I'll look into it, Ma."

"I'm doing a story now, not six months from now, and if you don't help me put a stop to that racket, I'll say so."

"Hey, Ma, what's the trouble? You mad at your old Marty?"

"Not at you, Marty, but at some things in this town that stink."

"The only smell I know of comes from the loading pens." He chuckled at his wit.

"Marty, if your city police keep gouging the

cowboys coming up the trail, pretty soon Opportunity won't get any more business."

"We're the top of the Chisholm trail, sweetheart. Where they gonna go?"

"To any place that treats 'em right."

There was some truth to it, but Marty Drum wasn't about to admit it to the editor of the weekly paper.

It was time to hand the old lady a morsel. "There might be a little more enthusiasm for buffaloing cowboys than's necessary, Ma. I'll just have a quiet word with Spade, and that'll take care of it."

She stared right through him. "You always say that and every time you talk me into not running a story, I regret it."

This was getting dicey, but Marty knew how to cool her ardor. Confession. Admit some minor peccadillos and hide the big tickets.

"Coffee, Ma?" He gestured toward a table. "I'll have some sent up."

His mother didn't reply, but did settle herself in a kitchen chair. Marty never cooked, not with a first-class restaurant one floor down. Her demeanor was irritating him.

"Look, Ma, this city operates on fines and licenses. You know that. You benefit along with every other merchant in town.

"You know who really pays the taxes? Saloon operators like me. I get hit with a hundred dollar city license every year, and so do the rest of the other sporting outfits. On top of that, I

27

pay a license on every green baize gaming table.

"Then there's the girls . . ." he let that one fade out. "The city also charges a dime a head to use its shipping pens, so we get a good chunk of our revenue there. Fifty thousand head a year, that's five thousand into the city coffers.

"The stockmen pay. The Texans pay. You know what it means? The paper makes a profit. You get ads from Ed Wilber's Mercantile, Billy de Vere's livery barn, Joe Pflug's blacksmith place. You get them ads, Ma, and you wouldn't if there was a mess of taxes. Maybe Spade's been nipping a bit much off them cowboys, and I'll just have a word with him."

He gave her the big hosanna-amen smile.

She didn't budge. "He cleaned the Waggoner crew out of every cent they had," she said. "I guess I'll hitch up and ride out to their camp for a little interview. You can expect a story."

"Hey, Ma, just hold off a few weeks. Shipping season's almost over. You do a story now, you'll just get everyone riled up."

She didn't reply and that meant he hadn't even made a dent in her plans. But maybe that was all right. Let Spade take some heat from the paper. It would keep attention away from other matters.

"Bo Waggoner died last night," she said. "By his own hand, I hear. A man spends three months driving cattle from south Texas to here, and sells them to McCoy, and when he dies there's not a cent on him."

"Yeah, that's some tragedy. Only it wasn't any

28

two thousand. They lost most of the herd, I hear. Big stampede into the Red during a hellacious storm, and a quarter drowned dead. And if that wasn't bad enough, them Jayhawkers down on the Kansas line held them up for a bunch. And then they ran into the quarantine — tick fever's bad this year — and them state men turned a bunch back, and old Bo, he gets up to Opportunity this year with hardly enough beef to pay his hands. No wonder he didn't want to go back home."

She stared. "I'll talk to Addison McCoy and get the shipping figures," she said.

"Aw, Ma, leave it lie. It'd just hurt those Waggoner boys all the more, writing stuff like that about their pa."

This was trouble with a capital T. The cattle broker would tell her that Bo Waggoner had sold over fifteen hundred mixed longhorns at eighteen a head, less a dollar commission for McCoy and three dollars shipping to Chicago, and that wasn't something he wanted his ma to find out.

"What happened to Waggoner's money?" she asked.

Marty grinned and shrugged. "Probably wired it."

"I'll ask," she said.

"You want to give Opportunity a black eye?"

"I want to report what's true."

He remembered to smile. "You're a great editor, Ma. Who'd ever think a woman could run a paper? You're the inspiration for everyone in town, keeping going like this, issue after issue. I guess you just won't rest on your laurels."

"Cut that out, Marty. I won't bury this story, not with a suicide, missing money, and everyone in the Waggoner outfit dead broke and dead silent. I talked to those boys last night, and there's a hell of a whole lot they're not telling me."

Marty remembered to smile, a big, bright, beaming grin that stretched across his kisser. He opened a window, and breezes played with a gauzy drape.

"Your heart's big as the whole prairie, Ma. But a little common sense might serve you here. You publish the wrong stuff, without getting it all checked out, and you could hurt Opportunity bad. So bad you might send those herds to some other town."

"I was hoping you'd help me get to the bottom of it."

"I'm helping every which way."

"Name one."

He laughed. "You're a pistol, Ma."

She didn't laugh. Instead, she pressed a hand on his. "It's not just me; it's the memory of your dad. It's his footsteps I'm walking in. You mostly remember him as an old drunk, but I remember the time when Gideon Drum kept towns right."

"Kept towns right?"

"That's what a fighting editor does. Keeps 'em right."

"Playing God, I'd say."

"That's not an editor's job. An editor gets the facts out, and lets the people judge."

He laughed. "All seventeen voters in Opportunity. I'll get myself shaved and go tell Spade Ball to lay off. That's all this is. The marshals don't get paid much, and they like to pad their income a bit. He's pocketing some loose change, and it don't help Opportunity none. In fact, it just lowers my bar receipts if those wild cowboys don't have nothing to spend in my place."

"Maybe," she said levelly.

She was onto him. Well, that wasn't so bad. She couldn't prove anything, and she hardly would start loading her type stick with words about her own son.

But the more he tried to persuade himself of that, the less likely it seemed. She might just take him on, and then there would be hell to pay.

"You go find out what you can, Ma, and then tell me. If you come up with something wrong around here, just let me know privately, and I'll deal with it, and you'll see me clean it up."

"Maybe, Marty," she said.

He didn't like that.

She stood. "You know, I came here for some news from the mayor of this town, thinking my son, my own boy, would want more than anything else to make things right in Opportunity. I hope I'm not jumping to wrong conclusions."

The silence stretched.

"Here's a deal, Ma. If there's a problem around here, I'll have it rooted out before the next edition, and you can quote me."

"Maybe I will," she said.

She eyed the closed bedroom door as she headed for the long stairwell down to the street.

"Those women are expensive and dangerous," she said.

Marty watched her descend. He had some things to do fast, and no time to waste.

CHAPTER 4

Joe Waggoner figured his brothers were waiting for him to make the decisions because he was the oldest. Dog and Ring were better at leading men, but somehow the burden fell to Joe, and he was not comfortable in those big boots.

But someone had to ramrod the outfit back to Texas. And someone had to see to it that Bo Waggoner was decently planted and make sure the outfit had some provisions. Fourteen men downed a heap of vittles and drank a flood of Arbuckle's.

They had camped, as usual, on the windy bedding ground south of the Little Arkansas River, and now the whole crew, fourteen in all, had collected there. That rotten marshal had let them all out of the pokey after cleaning out their pockets, including the lint.

Cookie was scraping the griddle. He had fried up some johnnycakes for breakfast, and now an odd silence had descended over the camp.

"Dog, Billy, let's go see about burying Pa," he said. "Ring, you stay here, move the camp over there a piece, maybe some better grass yonder, and wait."

He eyed the remuda unhappily. The only way

they could bury Pa and buy some groceries would be to peddle some good saddle stock. Some of the boys would walk to Texas, or ride that bone-jarring cook wagon with Cookie.

"Billy, put halters on the blaze sorrel, the grulla, and the one with three stockings," he said.

Ring helped the boy, and shortly, the sons of Bo Waggoner were riding to Opportunity, three miles distant. The town had erected a crude plank bridge across the river, and this time of year it was usually jammed with cattle being driven to the massive pens beside the railroad. That proved to be the case today. Some outfit was pushing longhorns over the bridge, which thundered under the hammering of so many hooves.

"I reckon I'll ask if we can slide in," he said, trotting his chestnut over to a cowboy lounging in his saddle. A U-Bar man, it turned out.

"Hey, Joe Waggoner here. You mind if we slip in?"

The cowboy shrugged. "Go easy, that's all."

Waggoner returned to his brothers. "Yeah, we can do it, but easy. String out them horses and slide in close to the bridge."

They negotiated the bridge in a sweaty moment, rubbing shoulders with the nervous longhorns, which were spooked by the thundering of hoof on wood. On the other side, Joe urged his horse into a trot and angled away from the U-Bar herd.

His goal was the whitewashed board-and-batten furniture store of Jasper Dill, who did a coffin business in a back room. The boys tied up at the hitchrail and trooped into the store, tromping past knotty pine tables and ash rocking chairs and a horsehair sofa until they reached a red velvet-curtained area.

Dill was in there, tapping finishing nails into a corner of a shellacked, yellow pine coffin.

"Waggoner," he said. "Just finishing up. I guess you boys just want a pine box, eh? I've got a walnut one. More respect for the departed."

"Pine," Joe said.

The brothers gathered around. Their pa lay on a copper-topped table, covered with a sheet. It wasn't much of a box for a man who owned a big chunk of the Hill Country of central Texas.

"What'll this cost?" Joe said.

Dill stared sharply at Joe, maybe calculating dollars from Joe's worn clothing.

"Fifteen for the coffin, fifty for a funeral, plot, and digging the grave."

"We'll want a good preacher."

"That's ten more. You want a stone?"

Something sad unloosed in Joe. "Maybe next year. Just a wood marker."

"When?"

"Sooner the better."

"It'll take Spuds and Howie time to dig. Maybe four o'clock?"

"All right, four."

"Seventy-five in advance."

35

"Damn you," Joe said. "You haven't an ounce of decency in you."

"Not an ounce," said Dill. "Now help me lay him in the box."

Seventy-five was a lot of money. Maybe they should just take Pa out of town and bury him on the prairie.

A few minutes later the Waggoner boys slipped out to their horses on Main Street and led the spares to the Big O Livery Barn.

"We have to get a hundred-fifty for these nags," Joe said. "Pa owed the Stockmen Hotel thirty-seven. And we gotta eat."

"They're worth more'n that," Dog said.

"Not to a livery man."

De Vere offered thirty apiece, after a quick tour of each horse and some chewing on a straw.

"Don't need lame horses," he said.

"They're not lame, and you'll sell sound horses in two days, what with all the Texans in town."

"Sorry, Waggoner, take it or leave it."

"We'll leave it. I can sell 'em myself on Lone Star Street," Joe said.

"Hey! You Texans think you can tell the whole world what to do."

Joe led his brothers to the cowboy side of town, which was cramped, gaudy, and noisy. They spread out, Joe to the cream and gilded Lone Star Saloon, Dog to the green-painted Oriental, Foley and Ring to the false-fronted barn-red Trail's End, and Billy over to the white

clapboard Palace Variety Hall, with a real mar-
quee hanging off its front.

An hour later they had a hundred seventy-two
dollars and fifty cents, and Joe had penned three
bills of sale. Texians knew good horse flesh,
even if Kansans didn't.

After Joe had paid the undertaker his seventy-
five dollars, they spent the afternoon dickering
with the merchants for trail supplies and then
headed for Dill's. He didn't have a proper
hearse, just a black-enameled wagon with that
yellow pine box in back and the preacher on the
seat beside him.

Joe and his brothers followed the wagon out
of Opportunity along a two-rut trail, heading toward a lonely knoll west of town. There wasn't a
cottonwood or a willow in sight; just sighing
grass and wimpering wind and a featureless sky,
cloudless and empty as eternity.

When they pulled up before an open grave in
the Opportunity Cemetery, they found they
weren't alone. One man in workmen's garb held
a shovel. Another was Addison McCoy, the
cattle broker and an associate of the Waggoners.
Joe was mighty glad to see him. Old McCoy
hadn't forgotten Pa.

And the other person was that newspaper
woman, Angie Drum. She was swathed in black,
as if she were a mourner instead of just a reporter grabbing a story. He stared at her,
wanting to chase her away. This suicide was
family business, not something for *The Opportu-*

nity Outlook. They hadn't even invited their own Texas crew.

But he discovered something in her face, her eyes, and he recognized it as caring, and saw that this thin, hard-used, graying woman radiated a strange beauty, concern in her face, her eyes, and her hands, which were clasped together.

Those luminous eyes beheld the Waggoner boys tenderly, like his ma's eyes had, and Joe glanced at his brothers to see whether they'd noticed. They had, and suddenly this wasn't a family affair, but something more, and the boys didn't know what to do or say except to stand on one bootheel or the other and look anywhere but at her, or at that chalky hole, or at the yellow pine box resting on the wagon.

Joe wished he'd shaved and washed up. What would she think of the Waggoners, coming to this moment in trail-worn clothing?

"Are we all present?" asked the high-domed preacher.

He peered about as they collected beside the grave. Joe nodded.

"I'm Wilson Seltzer, pastor over at the First Methodist church, and I'm here to bury this beloved father, fine cattleman, and noted Texas pioneer," he said. "And after I've led us through a little service, I'll invite any of you men to talk about your father if you want."

Joe didn't. Everything jammed too tightly in his breast, and he lacked words, and if he couldn't find words, his brothers would be worse. They could all put a bullet into a knot at thirty feet, but couldn't even stammer something simple, such as that Pa was a fine man.

The wind ruffled Wilson's hair as he spoke sonorously of death and life and hope and faith and everlasting peace. Joe didn't care much for the words; they slid into the wind and vanished, but he was glad Pa was getting properly buried here, in a place, and not on the trail, in no place at all. Maybe someday they could have him shipped down to Texian soil and laid beside Ma, where he belonged.

"Yea, though I walk through the valley of the shadow of death, I will fear no evil: for thou art with me," Wilson said, his Bible opened to the 23rd Psalm.

When it came time for a eulogy, the Waggoner boys declined, but Addison McCoy didn't. He stepped to the edge of the grave and eyed them warmly for a moment. Joe thought the man had a dignity about him that would have pleased Ma.

"Young men, I've known your father for six years. We met here when Opportunity was just being born. In all those years, we've done pure handshake business, each of us satisfied completely. I received cattle in fine shape because your father drove them well, found grass, and drifted them slow, and I count him as a great man, bone-down honest, the finest of the finest of Texas, and that's why I'm here. Just so you men know."

He went on like that for a few minutes, and Joe found himself thirsty for more. He wanted McCoy to talk like that for an hour and for the newspaper woman to record every word and run the entire story in her paper. He wanted uncaring Opportunity to know that a fine man had died, and that the entire damned Kansas town should have come to the funeral, and not just a reporter . . .

Joe, Dog, Foley, Ring, Billy, and McCoy wrestled the pine box to the graveside, and spastically lowered their pa into the cold earth, the canvas straps sliding through their fingers. Then the dominie committed the soul of Bo Waggoner to God and led them in a final prayer.

They all shook hands, then the minister rode off with Dill, while the newspaper woman climbed aboard McCoy's buggy.

"Mr. Waggoner," she said, "please stop at my paper. You and your brothers. I'd like to talk with you some more."

"Sure," Joe said. They wouldn't start south until dawn anyway.

The runny-nosed gravedigger was already piling chalky clay into that hole, where his pa would lie for eternity.

She smiled gently, and he felt her caring again.

CHAPTER 5

Angie seethed with questions. Why were the Waggoner boys so placid? Wouldn't they be angry? Threatening to tree the town? Why had nothing been done about the missing money? Why had no one from town, except Addison McCoy, come to bury Bo Waggoner? Bo and a dozen Texans like him were the lifeblood of Opportunity, and yet no one, including Marty, her son the mayor, had come to pay respects.

Maybe she would get some answers. She reached the newspaper before the Waggoner boys did and had scooped up a notepad and stubby pencil before they trooped in. She had told them she wanted to write an obituary; actually, she wanted much more, but she wasn't sure she would get it.

The Texans seemed in a hurry. Joe had herded them there, and his hold on them was shaky at best.

They lounged along the counter over which she transacted her daily business, peering solemnly at the grimy plant, the hulking Washington acorn press, the little job press, the caseboxes, the stacks of newsprint, the mounds of unsorted old issues, and a desk groaning under stratified bills, dunning notices, and exchange papers.

"I'm glad you came," she said. "Your father was an important man, and I want to do him justice. I'm going to write a good story, and I'll send a copy of it down there."

It was as if she were talking to a wall of penguins.

"Joe, how old was he?"

"Ah, fifty-one."

"Birthdate?"

"April eighteenth, eighteen and twenty-six. In Virginia; I don't rightly know where. Mountains somewhere."

"Survivors?"

"Us and little Andy, he's too young. Three died, two sisters and a brother."

"Your mother?"

"She passed away."

Expertly she collected all the vital statistics, survivors, dates, and places. They weren't reluctant to supply all that, but she wondered how she would fare with the rest.

"Your pa was a fine man."

Joe nodded.

"I hear he pioneered the Chisholm."

"Almost. He wasn't the first, but he shipped more beeves up it than any other Texian. And he did it with less trouble and loss than all the rest put together."

"How'd he do that, Joe?"

"Well, he wasn't typical."

"A typical Texan?"

"No, a typical man. There wasn't a cowhand in Texas who wouldn't work for him."

"Was it pay?"

"No, ma'am, he paid about the same as the rest. But he never yelled at a man, never blamed or scolded. Just a quiet word. Some thought he wasn't tough, and down there, ma'am, tough is the thing to be. But that doesn't mean he was soft. Hard to explain. Just a quiet word, and he'd get what he wanted. Men trusted him. He never lost a man on the trail, except the time a water moccasin bit one. That hit him hard."

"Your father was prominent, then?"

Joe flushed a little. "I don't pay mind to that. But every stockman and politician in Texas, they all came calling."

"You men admire him."

They laughed as if it had been a stupid question, and maybe it had. She could see it in these sons.

"This was a tough trip," she said.

Joe nodded.

"I heard you lost some cattle in river crossings."

"Red River flooding, yes, ma'am. And other things."

"Trouble in the Nations?"

"Night thieves, ma'am, five here, ten there."

"Jayhawkers, too, I hear."

Dog replied angrily. "They jumped us near the Kansas line, thirty of 'em. We was just breaking camp in the morning, quiet little green valley, and there they were. Some still wearing the federal blue, saying we were bringing tick fever up from Texas, and that hurt Kansas stockmen, and they wanted five hundred. Pa, he saw how it was, thirty-some ex-soldiers, all of them guns aiming at us.

"So Pa says he didn't fight against the Union, he was down in Mexico trying to make a ranch go in Chihuahua, but that didn't stop those Jayhawkers none, and they just laughed and began chowsing out their pick. They held us under gunpoint for half a day while they drove that bunch of longhorns out of there. Pa, he took it hard. We got taxes and fees and invoices needed paying up, and a land mortgage."

Angie wrote that quietly. "How many did you end up with?"

There was some bitterness in Joe's voice. "Fifteen hundred twenty-two, or some such. We tallied two thousand one nine six when we started."

Angie ached to ask a dozen questions, but the Waggoners were looking ready to bolt.

"McCoy give you a good price?"

"Fair enough, ma'am."

"Enough to pay off your crew and yourselves?"

"Pa never stints on that. Fast as he got greenbacks, he paid wages, and a bonus, too. We all got three months trail wage and a double eagle besides. We thought we'd have us a fine time,

44

and that first night after we sold the herd, he let half of us go to town. Other half had to hold the cows; it takes a few days to get stock cars in and pens cleared."

Angie pretty well knew what was coming next. Spade Ball and his deputies began their usual pocket-cleaning, finding excuses to throw the Waggoner men into the pokey. The usual deal was to run them over to the justice of the peace, Sid Wannamaker, who would fine them twenty and costs, or whatever they had in their pockets. City taxes, paid by Texans.

"Joe, let it go," Dog said.

Joe shut up. "Guess we'll go now, ma'am. You send us the notice about Pa."

"Boys, if you think the way the town shakes down the cowboys is news to me, you're mistaken. There's no taxes here. I don't pay a nickel property tax for this building," she said. "So they ran you through their tax mill. Did your pa have to bail any of you out?"

"They got him, too. He was just crossing the street, that's all, going back to the hotel after a supper, and this talking jawbone with a star pinches Pa and hauls him off, and next thing, Pa's in the justice court and it's eighty dollars for disturbing the peace."

Angie sighed. "Was he drinking?"

"Pa don't drink, hardly ever. He believes a man should set a good example, be upright, be a friend to all, and be wise enough to do the right thing."

"Is this worse than other years?"

"Lot worse," said Foley.

Angie gathered her nerve. "This why he . . ."

"No, ma'am, he didn't do it for that . . ."

"Let it go, Joe," Dog said.

"Maybe I can help," said Angie.

"You? The mayor's mother?"

She paused, trying to answer that in some way that these men would accept. "The paper's the only force in town capable of helping you and other Texans. Want to take a chance on me?" She met with the wall of silence again, but plowed ahead. She had nothing to lose. "Where'd the money go? Did any official of this town steal it? It that why your father put the gun to his head?"

"No, if they'd stole it all, we'd be treeing the town," Joe said. "Pa got behind; he needed to take a good year's profit back to Texas to pay the new mortgage and all the rest. Instead, he was six thousand in the hole after he'd sold to McCoy, so he thought maybe to play some faro. We told him, don't do that, what does he know about that?"

"Faro, here?"

"Lone Star Saloon, ma'am. Trouble is, Pa's not one of them you see so much in Texas, poker players, whiskey sippers, not cut from that cloth at all. But he knew faro's mostly square, odds are almost even, hard for a dealer to cheat, pulling one card at a time out of a slit in a box like that . . ."

46

"So Bo Waggoner played to win it back."

"We pretty near were shouting at him, ma'am, because he's just a sheep waiting for a shearing. But he went ahead, laid out some greenbacks for five-dollar chips, and started in laying down chips on the oilcloth. It looked good for a while there, mighty fine, and his pile grew some, and we were begging him to pack up and go, even if he wasn't out of trouble all the way. He just smiled and shook his head. They kept trying to get him to have some whiskey, this woman with a lot of creamy skin showing, and finally he took a drink or two. Then after he'd won a big pile, they put a new dealer on that table . . ."

"I guess I know the rest of the story," Angie said.

"It sure didn't take long, that new dealer winning it all back. Pa went broke and wandered across to the hotel and that was the last time we saw him alive," Joe said.

"It was too much for him," Ring muttered.

"Was he cheated?"

They looked at one another and at the floor. Joe finally volunteered. "Don't honestly know. Not so any of us could see. We was all watching that grease-hair dealer, mad at Pa for not cashing in and getting to bed. He just got stubborn and wouldn't quit."

Angie had, at last, an inkling why these sons didn't threaten to tear Opportunity apart. By their reckoning, their pa had brought the disaster on himself. She wasn't so sure. Even faro could be manipulated by a clever card mechanic. Maybe by one of the dealers in Marty's emporium. Maybe at Marty's request. She felt a wave of shame.

"What's going to happen now?" she asked, softly.

Joe shrugged. "Waggoner ranch's done for. It goes to the bank in Austin. We have some young stock we didn't drive, mostly breeders, but the creditors will snap that up. Pretty hard to start over now. No more scrub cattle running in the brush, like there was after the War of Secession. We don't know what we'll do. Maybe hire on with other outfits."

"Your pa was a strong man. I don't really know why he would . . . end it. Strong men find ways to start over."

"He had a bowel cancer, doc told him so. He was doing this last drive for us, and it went bad. So he cashed in."

"He deserved better. He deserved to have every official in this town, every merchant in this town, paying their respects. But no one came, except one."

"We noticed that, Miz Drum. We ain't coming back."

CHAPTER 6

Angie watched the Waggoner boys troop out. It had been a long and painful day for them, and she didn't want to press them further. The interview had answered most of her questions. She had wondered why the Waggoner boys hadn't threatened to rip Opportunity up and scatter the remains across the prairie, and now she knew.

Opportunity wasn't the sole cause of their misfortune, except in some small way. The Jayhawkers down in the Nations had stolen a quarter of their herd. And their pa had foolishly tried to make it up at the faro layout.

But that didn't mean that Opportunity was without blame. The whole law and justice system in town was a thinly disguised tax operation, milking the drovers and cattlemen as ruthlessly as possible.

The town licensed saloons, cribs, variety shows, and each gambling table, all for a fancy price. And its constables ran hapless drovers into the calaboose with no excuse at all, and either sent them to the justice court to be mulcted for allegedly disturbing the peace, or else the pocket cash of these newly paid cowboys ended up in some local tills. She wondered whose.

She would write a good obituary for a man she admired. But she wondered what to put in it. And she wondered whether some things ought to go into a separate story. It wouldn't be an easy decision. Marty would probably storm in if she even hinted that things were amiss. She didn't want that.

She didn't even want to tell the world that Bo Waggoner went broke at an oilcloth-covered table in Marty's emporium. She didn't think her son had chosen a proper calling, but who was she to run his life? It was good that he was mayor. She had supported him, written of his admirable qualities, endorsed him, and got him into office.

He was her only living child, and that shot pangs of feeling through her. He wasn't a bit like her, and even less like Gideon; more carefree, less worn and worried, more optimistic, probably better at running a business. She and Gideon had always wrestled with a thousand ethical beliefs that didn't much disturb Marty. Maybe she was too concerned about doing right.

For Marty she felt a cautious love. She didn't know where the wariness came from; only that something in him troubled her, though she tried hard to overcome it. He was a good son. Whenever some businessman or local rancher came storming at her paper, he sprang to her defense. *The Outlook* was protected by the mayor, by the marshals, and by the city justice court. So she loved him, and sometimes wondered what it was that softly cautioned her, like a patch of mysterious fog on a brilliant summer day. And he loved her . . . she thought.

She put off writing the obituary until she had done a little reporting. The rest of that morning she spent talking with Addison McCoy about the number of longhorns he had purchased from Waggoner and what he had paid for them. Then she walked over to the board-and-batten house of Justice Wannamaker, who sometimes conducted the court in his front parlor when he didn't feel like walking over to the pine-paneled courtroom in the fieldstone city hall. Marty had erected that hall on Kansas Street across from Marty's other big project: a secure jail.

The judge had no clerk, and he himself entered each offense, date, and fine in a big buckram-bound ledger. She copied off a few figures while he glared. But the mayor's mother had certain privileges. Then she stopped at the jailhouse, a mortared limestone and iron strap affair. The front half housed the Opportunity police force. Spade Ball wasn't around, and his scanty records weren't in sight.

She sighed, walked back to her shop, and headed for the composing table. She decided to set the obituary without writing it out beforehand. She knew what she wanted to say. It saved time to avoid one stage of the process, and she was getting better and better at composing while her stained fingers deftly plucked up the letters from their tiny cubicles and slid them backward and upside down into the type stick.

She sure needed help, and if the paper got much bigger she would have to find someone: a compositor, an ad salesman, an accountant. Anyone who could relieve her brutal toil. Even now, she spent fourteen or fifteen hours a day, seven days each week, wrestling the paper to life, and then wrestling it back into type in a casebox.

She began with the brief description of the funeral, since word of Waggoner's suicide had long since circulated through Opportunity. She took pains to list those present, with Addison McCoy figuring prominently. Maybe that would shame those predatory shopkeepers who had enjoyed Waggoner's patronage for years, but couldn't hie themselves up the hill to bid the man who had enriched them all good-bye.

Then she turned to the big, bluff, gentle-mannered Texan who had the courage to drive longhorns five hundred miles to the railroad, braving storms, stampedes, constant danger, and robbers. He wasn't like his boisterous fellow Texans, she said; Bo Waggoner had a quieter nature, but imposed a sterner discipline on himself and his drovers. All his men loved and trusted him, not least his many sons.

She described how his string had run out: bowel cancer, one last drive, theft in the Nations, brutal treatment by the illegal and vicious

Jayhawkers, predatory army veterans who refused to settle down.

Then she came to the crossroad she dreaded: whether to write about the treatment his outfit received in Opportunity or not. Whether to displease plenty of people or not. Whether to cause trouble for Marty or not.

She set down the type stick. The lines of type had accumulated to twelve inches in the galley tray, and she was nearing the end of her story. Each of those lines of metal letters was separated by leading, a thin sheet of typemetal that put some white space, or "air" between it and the other lines of type.

That column of metal was the story, and it had been growing inch by inch through the morning. How innocuous it looked, a rectangle of dull metal forming a sheet of words. Yet no story was ever innocuous, and once all those lines were inked and paper pressed into them, that long block of metal letters, so tediously assembled, could trigger passions, start riots, comfort the afflicted, win an election or sway a trial.

She chose to say a little. It was germane. She probably would regret it.

"Waggoner's hands had an unusually rough time in Opportunity," she wrote. "The first night after payday, five of them were pinched by Marshal Ball, charged with disturbing the peace, and taken the next morning before Justice of the Peace Sid Wannamaker, who fined each of them $20 and costs. The nature of the infractions is unknown.

"The next day, according to Waggoner's sons, the marshal rounded up seven others, including two Waggoner boys, held them overnight, charged them with nothing, but relieved them of all their cash. Waggoner had been forced to give them each a ten dollar advance against wages to help them purchase gear for their return to Texas. It has not been ascertained what offense these trail-weary boys were accused of, if any."

Oh, that one would stir up a storm. Everyone in town knew it was happening, but no one had ever seen it in print. She expected Spade Ball to throw a fit.

Then she went light on Marty. "The stockman, his resources seriously depleted and unable to cover mortgage and other debt from the proceeds of this year's drive, chose to repair his fortunes with an unusual measure, at least for him. He began playing faro at a local resort about six that evening and initially saw his diminished stake gain ground until he was three thousand dollars ahead.

"The resort plied him with free whiskey, which he drank reluctantly, and then freely. But when a new dealer took over, Waggoner's fortunes waned steadily. Ignoring the entreaties of his sons, he continued to play into the night until he had exhausted all of his resources. Mr. Waggoner was neither a drinker nor a gambler.

"Before midnight, after losing everything, he

abandoned the resort, went to his hotel, and discharged a Colt's revolver into his head, dying instantly. He was discovered at once, and Marshal Ball declared the matter a suicide."

Well, there it was. She didn't mention the Lone Star Saloon or Marty. As far as any reader might know, the gambling debacle might have occurred anywhere in town that night. Marty was smart. He would understand the favor, and next time she saw him he would grin at her the way he always did, and maybe wink.

She would do that for Marty anytime, even if it bothered her some. She thought of it as more than a mother's love; her treatment of Marty's administration was a favor, and all news people needed to call in their favors now and then. She was obligating Marty.

When she had finished the typesetting, she inked the column in the galley tray with a porous roller and laid a long sheet of newsprint over the story. Then she proofed it, trying not to sully her fingers in the sticky proofing ink. She saw no typos, but some cropped up anyway every time she plucked a finished paper from the freshly printed pile and read it. She supposed she needed spectacles.

Then she carried the galley to a composing stone, a portable metal table where a chase, or page form, rested. She would fit the obituary into the front page later. She wasn't happy with it. She worked at other things, setting some ads, church news, some material about the price of wheat, and a drought in Montana.

By afternoon, she would have some baking news from Mrs. Danzig, some weekly cattle prices from McCoy, and some telegraphic news from Oglesby at the train station. The paper was filling out. She thought she would run some filler this time. No one had any idea what it took out of her to print a weekly paper, even a four-page one, month after month, with never a break or a vacation.

Thursday and Friday she sold ads and tried to collect from merchants. Half the time they begged off, or complained that they lacked cash, or wanted to barter something for the price of an ad. Sometimes they enraged her, poor-mouthing in the middle of the bonanza time of year, when outfit after outfit from Texas drifted in and cleaned off their shelves, shelling out hard cash. But Gideon had warned her that a quarter of what was owed for advertising would never be collected, so she had to set the price of ad space to cover the losses.

She spent Sunday doing her books and pre-paring subscription notices. These she would put in the mail on Monday, and old Horatio Bates, the postmaster of Opportunity, would cancel the stamps and poke them into the right boxes. Monday and Tuesday she would set more type and pull together the four pages. And then, on Wednesday, she would print the next edition of *The Opportunity Outlook* and start the whole thing over again.

CHAPTER 7

Mayor Martin Drum did not like to be rousted from bed before eleven. Nothing short of an earthquake would excuse the invasion of his bedroom, he had often said.

So maybe there was an earthquake. He awakened to a pitiless hammering on his door. Only one person had a mean fist like that: City Marshal Spade Ball. Drum shook the erotic dreams out of his skull, shrugged into his burgundy silk robe with yellow piping, and padded toward the shivering, four-panel, white-enameled door, wondering whether it would survive the assault.

"This better be good," he said to the looming presence at his threshold.

The marshal steamed in and stuffed a copy of the flimsy four-page *Outlook* into the mayor's wine-colored silken belly.

"Nothing in any paper published in Kansas is worth waking me up," the mayor said, seizing it and poking his face into various stories.

Ball waited, exuding menace.

The front-page Waggoner story caught Drum's eye. What was it, an obituary or a news item? He read slowly. Without a dose of java,

57

slow was the only way he could digest so much as a school primer.

Ball remained silent, stabbing a fat trigger finger at the paper as if to poke holes in it.

Most of the story seemed innocuous. The venue of Waggoner's financial ruin remained delicately unspoken. His mother would never spill the beans. Nary a word about the Lone Star Saloon and Gaming Emporium, same address, one floor below.

But other items in the story evoked a rush of heat. One was the clear assertion that the Waggoner crew had been railroaded through the justice court for no good reason. Worse, the story said that Marshal Spade Ball had wantonly thrown some of these innocents into the city jail, neglected to charge them with any violation of city ordinances, much less violations of the canon of Kansas or God, and cleaned their pockets.

It looked bad. In fact, it was a painfully public proclamation that the heap of meat standing in Drum's parlor was a crook. The mayor wished he could remember the various terms for that sort of dark profiteering. Peculation, no; absconding, no; graft? Well, whatever it was, bright, shining, Kansas daylight had come upon it.

The thing is, everyone in Opportunity knew it and ignored it. But putting something like that into print, in a newspaper circulating everywhere in the county and out to other exchange

papers, was dark magic, and suddenly important.

"Damn her," he grumbled.

"I'm gonna shut her down, libeling a lawman
like me." Spade Ball stabbed air with his trigger
finger.

"No, you aren't. You're leaving my mother
alone."

"Try and stop me."

"You try it, and you're fired."

"Maybe I won't quit."

Ball was sounding like he had some allies on
the city council. But it was all bluster.

"Spade, cool off. Let me handle it. She just
took leave of her senses, and I'll make sure the
next issue patches it up. Meanwhile, if you want
to avoid trouble, quit shaking down the cowboys. Run 'em through court, like we want. The
loot belongs to the city."

"You pay me three hundred a month, and I'll
run 'em through court. Sixty dollars don't make
a living. Meanwhile, I'm going to separate their
greenbacks from their purses any way I can. You
and Sid Wannamaker, you'll get plenty for the
city and your own deep pockets."

Marty turned statesman, just like President
Rutherford Birchard Hayes. "Next thing you
know, Spade, them trail outfits will be heading
for some other town like Abilene, Newton, or
anyplace on the rails that treats 'em better."

Ball laughed. "Progressive Mayor Drum,
seeing the future. I'll tell you the future. In

three, four years, Opportunity won't see any more Texas beef, dead or alive. They're building rails in Texas. Chisholm Trail's getting fenced with bobwire. Wheat farmers settling in here, and before you know they'll shut down Lone Star Street, and you'll be selling sarsaparilla and feeling good to clear fifty bucks a month.

"And what'll Opportunity be? A crossroads selling bonnets to farm wives and worming powder to farmers. Your ma's paper, it's gonna fold, fewer and fewer merchants with ads, and subscribers walking away, too. You get the message?"

Drum did. But he and others had a remedy for it: petition Kansas to carve out a new county and turn Opportunity into its seat. A paper could survive on legals in a county seat, and he could prosper running a few saloons and private poker clubs for the county commissioners. But that would have to wait until the cattle business died down. A wide-open town was the only way to keep the beef money in Kansas.

"Spade, you just go mind your business. I'll have a word with her. She just wasn't thinking."

"She was thinking. She kept you out of it. Everyone knows how much Waggoner lost downstairs. She's just picking on me, and by God, I'll deal with it."

The trigger finger was stabbing sunlight again.

"She's got notions about the law enforcement around here, and not much I can do to stop her.

60

She thinks you shouldn't pick on those cowboys."

"Well, there's plenty I can do. She ain't my mother. Remember that."

"As mothers go, I have the better of you."

"Every mother's son on earth got the better of me. But I'll tell you what's going to happen to yours if I see one more word about me in that rag. Her fonts are going to end up in the river. Every last vowel and consonant. And her press, it's going to end up scrap metal. If she don't stop writing libelous stories about me, I'll shut her up so tight she'll never write another word."

"It's just female sentiment. She likes cowboys."

Ball hooted. "Likes cowboys! Let me tell you something, Mayor Drum, visionary of the future of Opportunity. I'm doing the Texans a favor. Putting their money to good causes, keeping Opportunity awash in revenue. There's not a merchant pays a nickel in taxes, thanks to me."

His jabbing finger seemed to slice the sunlight into pieces.

"You know what a cowboy is?" the marshal continued. "He's solid bone between two ears. It's called unskilled labor. No man in his right mind would be a cowboy if he could do something better. Everything a cowboy knows can be taught in two days. That's why they get twenty a month and found. Twenty and found!

"Who else would be dumb enough to follow

the ass-end of cows for three months, living outside, catching catarrh, eating rotten chow with sand in it, too dumb to get out of the rain? So they can throw a rope. So what? The average cowboy's the stupidest critter in the stable."

He was jabbing that lethal digit again.

"The proof of it's right in front of our eyes. Do those rummies sock their pay away and take it back and buy a herd of their own? No, they blow it on booze and tarts and go home broke and in debt, telling themselves it was worth it. Can you dispute that?"

The mayor agreed. He shrugged.

"I thought so. Don't give cowboys no sympathy. They're dumber than the beeves they herd."

Marty Drum was growing tired of all this windy opinionizing. "All right, watch your step, and I'll have a little talk with Ma. Now don't ever get me up for anything less than Judgment Day."

"Watch my step?" This time Ball's finger jabbed into Drum's chest with a hard thump.

"Get smart and get rich," the marshal said and wheeled out the door. Drum heard his boots hammering wooden stairs.

It was suddenly very quiet, and, were it not for the wild frenzy of dust motes in the sun, the mayor would have thought of it as a sleepy morning.

Not a good way to start a day.

He was an old hand at limning his mother's

62

sensibilities, so he reread the obituary. He needed to understand perfectly if he wished to deal with her without causing a ruckus.

Waggoner's death was tragic, but he'd brought it on himself. He had thrown his money onto the table, making crazy bets, most over the house limit, but Marty's dealer, Deuce, knew where the pot would end up, and let him. Marty had corraled over twenty-three grand that golden night. He was rich. The greenbacks and double eagles choked his safe.

She plainly didn't like the town's mode of raising revenue, licensing sin and hornswaggling cowboys, but she had no quarrel there. Every cattle town on the railroads did it. Wichita, Abilene, Newton, none of them had levied a property tax, and never would as long as Texas drovers would pay the cost of government.

She knew too much, though, and that was a danger when mixed with her rectitude. One of the things that always concerned her was justice. If cowboys were being rung into the calaboose on trumped up charges, then the law and justice were both being traduced, and that would be more than enough to start her crusading. It wouldn't matter to her that the cowboys expected it and didn't mind, or that she herself paid not one cent of taxes.

He was going to have to check her. He could smell Virtue in that obituary. She was primed and ready to go on a rampage, and her targets were going to be the whole administration, Justice of the Peace Wannamaker, and especially Spade Ball and his deputies, the forty-four caliber engines of income for Opportunity. He was lucky to have Ball, the most formidable of all Western lawmen, a living legend, keeping the peace.

He belched sourly and poured tepid water from the pitcher into his basin. He would try to come up with an angle while he scraped his stubble. Then he would fortify himself with some java and head over to the paper and put some heat on the old lady.

He was pretty sure he could. He knew his ma better than anyone else on earth did, and he'd jolly her into a good mood and get her to promise to lay off. If he failed, he would have to find some way to get a little rough. Not hurt her, of course, but just let her know she was playing with fire when she was poking around the wallets of the mayor, the councilmen, the judge, and the law, not to mention a few merchants whose bread was buttered by the little green Tammany that ran Opportunity.

CHAPTER 8

Angie lugged fifteen copies of the new paper over to the post office on Second Street, hoping not to get snared by the postmaster, Horatio Bates. She didn't have time to listen to garrulous old Bates. Give him a minute, and he'd commandeer an hour.

Bates was her prize source of news, but he could also stupefy her with village-idiot observations. She felt the tropical air dampen her chest, and envied men, who could wear much less chest armor than women.

Endless toil had burned every ounce of fat from her, and she had wasted away so much that people worried about her health. Actually, she liked the flat planes of her face, her flesh barely veiling bone, and she thought her sculpted features were an asset. Not that she would even consider a man. She had had a surfeit of marriage and was glad to be on her own. And no other man could match Gideon, in spite of his weakness.

The bundle in her arm consisted of exchange papers, destined for other Kansas publishers, who shot her copies of theirs in return. That was how state and national news drifted in. They were free to print her stories, and she picked up good news from the exchanges that she perused each week, hunting the bizarre.

She discovered the postal tycoon, Horatio, selling one-cent green George Washingtons to Millicent Kowalski. Bates was fat-fingering a sheet of stamps, and was given to great deliberation in his every act and every utterance. The transaction would take awhile.

And yet she didn't mind. Her best stories and her deepest insights into Opportunity came from Bates, who somehow knew the nature of every reprobate and saint in town. Well, that's what postmasters do. They know everyone.

At last Millicent retreated, and Angie gratefully settled the bundle on the battered counter.

"Ah, Angie, the exchanges. Fifteen as usual? Let me see, here," he said, swiftly counting. "A very fine issue," he added. "I read mine over Arbuckle's this morning. *The Outlook* and coffee keep me regular."

He smiled benignly. That was the Bates version of a witticism.

"Forty-five cents," he said, scribbling a receipt. "Yes indeed, an obituary that will startle the local scalawags into running like scalded cats. Including hizzoner, I'd wager."

His eyebrow lifted.

She smiled, too smart to get sucked into this. She dug out four bits, and he made change. Often there was no coin in Opportunity, and then he wrote her a chit, or sold her stamps.

"In the middle of an obituary, you threw light upon illegal acts done by the constables sworn to uphold the law, and just for good measure described a racket by which sojourning Texans are bilked by our esteemed city court without the slightest pretense of serving justice, so that the cowboys can pay our city taxes for us. Very entertaining, Angie."

"Nothing will come of it," she said. "Would you get my mail out of the box?"

He did, handing her four exchange papers and some bills.

"Ah, Angie, you were more discreet discussing the faro game at the Lone Star. Somehow your son's establishment didn't get mentioned, although the fortune Bo Waggoner lost there was probably the last straw for the man. Ten minutes after he went broke in the Lone Star, I gather, he forcefully drove several grains of lead through his head."

"Horatio, you just mind your own damned business."

She fumed her way back to the paper. That mugwump! Maybe she'd write Washington City and try to lasso a less meddlesome postmaster. What she said or didn't say about Marty in print was her own business . . .

Or was it? She had concealed the locale of Waggoner's debacle to protect Marty; she couldn't deny that. She'd bent her principles. Well, that's what mothers were for, bending principles. She wasn't going to air the family's dirty linen. Gideon would have published the whole story, every last bloody scrap of it, but she wasn't Gideon.

She donned her printing smock and began breaking down the expired classified ads, pulling out the leading and then pitching the letters back into their little nests. She worked mindlessly, the distribution of the type so automatic that she didn't concentrate on the task.

Her thoughts strolled through everything she knew about the town's venal justice system, and she realized that a decision was looming: to publish more about the graft, or ignore it as she had all along. To wound her son's administration and maybe destroy his political career, or to let it slide.

She chose then and there to let it slide — publicly. For now. *The Outlook* might remain mum, but Marty was going to get an earful. Hell held no terror like an irate mother. Before she was done with Marty and his cabal of leeches, she was going to see change in the administration of Opportunity.

The decision wasn't so hard, really.

She threw the last capital *A* into the upper case and washed her stained hands again. She wondered whether she, like Lady MacBeth, was trying to scrub away sin. She wondered where her own sense of sin came from. She hadn't been religious. She hadn't violated the ordinary canons of virtue. And yet she saw her ink-purpled fingers as a metaphor for whatever pain her paper wrought in others. Anyone who had ever edited a newspaper knew that publishing news causes hurts. Editors have dirty hands.

She penned some advertising invoices, stuffed them into envelopes, gathered up proof copies of the new edition, and plunged into the hazy afternoon light. Every advertiser would receive a copy of the issue that bore the ad as proof of publication, along with a bill. That included the Lone Star Saloon. Marty had always been faithful with his advertising, usually hawking Cuban cigars, Tennessee whiskey, pretty serving girls, and Chicago variety acts.

She decided to go there first. She preferred to invade the Lone Star in the bright afternoon, when it lay supine, the harsh sunlight rebuking its habitués, and she didn't have to witness the tarts trolloping redeye to fuzzy-cheeked cowboys, and the consumptive card mechanics euchring boys of fifteen just up the trail from Kerrville or New Braunfels.

She found him in his windowless cubicle posting his ledger by lamplight. His black strongbox, with the pink cherubs on the door, had been opened, and within lay stacked trays of eagles and double eagles, plus some fat packets of greenbacks. The amount amazed her. She was seeing an enormous pile of cash on that shelf. Maybe Bo Waggoner's cash.

"Well, surprise," he said.

"Here's your proof copy and invoice."

"Nice paper, Ma, except for that obituary."

"I thought you'd be pleased. I left the Lone Star out of it."

"Oh, that was to be expected. But the rest . . ."

"You didn't like what I printed about Spade Ball."

He pursed his lips and grinned.

"Marty, I've come to tell you something. Now listen. Unless this petty graft stops, right now, I'm going to start telling tales in print."

"What petty graft?"

"Cut that out, Marty. The Waggoner boys and their crew were rounded up for no good reason, held overnight, never charged, and let loose in the morning after Spade had cleaned out their pockets."

"So? We don't pay him enough."

"I taught you better."

"Maybe he went easy on 'em. Maybe if he'd charged them, taken them over to Sid Wannamaker, he'd have fined them a hundred apiece and ten days jail."

She snorted. Why was Marty shrugging it off?

"What did the Flying W crew do? Disturb the peace? No. Public intoxication? No. Discharge a firearm in the city? No. Resist arrest? Start a brawl? Assault and battery? Destroy property? Piss in an alley? None of that. They happened to be Texans, and this town's picking on Texans for a living."

Marty grinned. "Beats taxes."

"That's no answer."

"Yes it is. You pay property taxes? Do Ed Wilber or Billy De Vere or Joe Pflug? Nosirree. The only ones who fork out city taxes are suckers like me. Saloon licenses. Gaming table licenses. I pay your taxes, but I get them back from the cowboys."

She glared at him. "You put a mechanic at the table when Waggoner started to win big. That's what I hear."

Marty shrugged. "Waggoner should've quit when he was ahead."

"I hear your tarts had ryed and ginned him all that evening. No doubt because you told them to."

"So? He drank them."

"Why didn't you step in? Tell Bo Waggoner to cash in and go to bed?"

"It's a free country, Ma. I let him do what he wanted."

"And now he's dead."

"He pulled the trigger."

"How much did you win from him?"

He shrugged slyly.

"I hear Bo Waggoner lost eighteen or twenty thousand dollars in here. And now it's in that safe."

"All by himself, Ma."

She stared at this grinning son of hers, seeing cheek she didn't like. His faro mechanic had cheated a cattleman out of a small fortune. Maybe Marty had always been like this. Maybe she'd been blinding herself. He was smoothly

71

denying that he had had anything to do with Waggoner's suicide.

"We both know better," she said.

"Them Texans, they're a bunch," he said. "Wild crowd coming here all summer, tearing Opportunity apart, blowing holes in the walls, breaking glass, scaring good people half to death. You know what I pay just for glass? Ma, when they cut loose, this whole town's in danger. Spade, he's just cooling them down overnight. He's the best in the lawing business. Maybe his jailhouse fines are a little informal, but they're necessary."

He beamed. She hadn't even made a dent.

"All right, Marty, *The Outlook*'s going to start exposing this stuff. I'd do almost anything not to get into a tussle with you, but we're going to make some changes here."

He stared up at her, then smirked. She'd seen that smirk a thousand times. It was cocky and deliberate. "You're right, Ma. We need some reform around here. You just hang on, hold off on them stories, and see me fix it. Watch what I do, not what I say. I'll wrestle Spade into being careful."

"Sorry, Marty, this time that won't do," she said.

She didn't let him smile his way out of it that time. She walked out of his dark lair, through the harsh-lit saloon, past a dull-eyed Chihuahua doxie perched on a battered bar stool, and into sunlight.

CHAPTER 9

Those thunderheads, the color of a bad bruise, boiling out of the west worried Addison McCoy. His yellow slicker rested under the buggy seat, but that offered no comfort. A judgment-day storm out on the open prairie could sure separate the sheep from the damned.

It wasn't just the torture of being pelted by icy rain, which had a way of rivering down his neck under the slicker and numbing his hands as he drove. He swore every time he got caught in one of those deluges that God was stalking him, pitching blue bolts left and right and forward and back, mocking his dwindling courage. Usually the horse shied and ran, sometimes shattering the buggy.

Once, just as he was approaching a herd that was charged with galvanic energy, he got caught in a stampede; the wild-eyed cattle terrorized by the crack and boom, the fox fire dancing on their horns, the clack of bone against bone rattling like rifle volleys, whipping madly by him as he cowered behind a benevolent copse of cottonwoods.

But for the moment the world seemed safe enough, and those black clouds sulked thirty miles distant. The air didn't satisfy his lungs, though, and evoked foreboding in him. Each shipping season he had driven out to the herds as they closed on Opportunity, sometimes meeting them ten or fifteen miles south of town on open Kansas prairie to dicker with the trail bosses.

He wasn't alone. His rivals hastened out to meet the herds, too, and cut a deal whenever they could. If McCoy had become the premier cattle broker in Opportunity, it was simply because of his attention to detail and not because he always bid the highest price.

McCoy could write a check on the spot, thanks to a substantial line of credit at the Merchant Bank, and paid the trail bosses in any way they wanted the money: cash, gold, letter of credit, transfer of funds, all at once or over time.

He received daily telegraphic reports from the stockyards in Kansas City, St. Louis, Chicago, and Memphis. He was better at getting stock cars delivered to the Opportunity siding on time. He had an instinct about cattle, and knew with a glance how healthy they were and whether they were gaining or losing weight. He even had an arrangement with a rancher north of town to pasture sick animals until they could be shipped or shot.

So most of the trail bosses working up the Chisholm dealt with him.

He was riding now to meet Will Whittle's outfit. He usually knew in advance who he would be dealing with because cowboys on the trail knew what outfits were ahead and what were behind, and sometimes they even visited with one another en route. Like the other cattle brokers in town, McCoy made careful inquiry. He had bought Whittle's herds before, and liked the man.

Today, as he drove the sweating trotter southward, he eyed the turf carefully. This deep into the trail season the grass would be well mauled by the several herds that had swept over it. The Chisolm ran miles wide, sometimes twenty or thirty miles wide, as each outfit tried to steer its beeves to fresh grass.

He didn't like what he saw. The denuded trail showed bare earth, and cattle arriving in town would be losing weight. Maybe one or two of those awesome storms would freshen things up, but that wasn't likely.

He liked to ship the first herds arriving in town, because they were fat and gaining weight, and suffered less shipping loss. Whittle's herd probably would be different, and he'd eye it carefully, looking for subtle hollows at the flank, caved in croups, and restlessness. Fat cattle settled down and chewed their cud all night. Hungry ones milled.

Mid-afternoon he drove to the crown of a hill and at once spotted the herd several miles to the southeast. All he saw, actually, was a golden haze, but that was the only clue he needed. He let the sweating horse rest. White foam had collected around the withers and on its stifles. He was far from water.

An hour later he could see the animals separately and distinctly and the point riders as well as one or two riders on the near flank. The breeze had stopped altogether, and the air lay sullen and oppressive. The clouds to the west had vaulted and darkened alarmingly. Instinctively, McCoy studied the terrain for shelter, perhaps a good cutbank that might keep him and his horse and buggy out of lightning's way. But this sea of grass offered little comfort, and he sensed that he might have a bad night.

He chose to wait. The herd would flow right past the knoll and probably camp a mile north on Dry Creek, which might have a few spring-fed puddles still standing. By August the rivulet usually played out.

They saw him now, and a horseman broke from the flank and rode toward him. Probably Whittle himself. McCoy's black buggy was a well-known emblem to cowboys riding toward Opportunity. He and Whittle could get right down to dealing.

He guessed twenty-five hundred longhorns, but one of his weaknesses was estimating the size of these herds. He's been fooled so many times he had learned just to wait and see. He swore that herds looked smaller when a keen wind whipped away the golden dust; larger when a vast crawl of dark animals blurred their way through choking plumes of grit.

It was Will Whittle, all right, riding a sweat-blackened grulla, the man's armpits stained, his red shirtfront caked with grime.

"It's you. Figured it would be," Whittle said, drawing up beside the buggy.

McCoy sprung out, feeling his years in his stiff legs, and shook hands. "How was the drive?" he asked.

"All right until we run out of grass a few days ago," the trail boss said. "Now they're caving in."

"We'll see," McCoy said. "Look like a goodly outfit from here." He handed the boss a canteen, and the cattleman poured water down his parched gullet.

"How are prices?" Whittle asked, returning the canteen.

"Not good. Height of the season. Eighteen and a quarter in Chicago, sixteen flat in KC."

"What about shipping?"

"Three a head; we're holding cattle in the pens an average of two days because the railroad's backlogged."

"Two days! That's ten pounds."

McCoy nodded.

They talked awhile while McCoy eyed the passing herd carefully. "How many?" he asked.

"Eighteen hundred some."

"Trail loss?"

"Those goddamned Jayhawkers."

"Sick?"

"Too damned many pregnant cows."

"Any steers?"

"None. All wild stuff."

McCoy grunted. That was going to cost Whittle. "Who's behind you?"

"Sandy Killhorn, three days. The Lazy H after that, out of San Marcos. After that I don't know. But I hear Hash Brown's two, three weeks back, with two herds."

McCoy drew a breath. "Hash Brown? Coming here?"

"That's what I hear. Your guess is as good as mine."

"Big herds?"

"The word is forty-five hundred in two bunches a day apart."

McCoy sighed. He had never met Brown and counted himself fortunate because of it. The man hadn't done a dime of legitimate business since the war. He had bullmoosed his neighbors off their ranges down there west of Alice, in southern Texas; locked horns with every land-owning male within a hundred-mile radius. And he always won.

His way of bargaining was to name his own price — monstrously low or high, depending on whether he was seller or buyer — and if the other party didn't agree, Brown would pound or threaten or kidnap or steal from the man until he caved.

He was known and dreaded by every cattle broker in Kansas, and most of the cattlemen in Texas, some of whom had put a price on Brown's head. But Brown had survived seven shootings, so the story went, and was likely to survive more.

"I'm glad I'll be out of here by the time Brown rolls in," Whittle said.

McCoy grunted.

Whittle tied his tired cowhorse to the buggy and hopped aboard.

"Want to look over the herd tonight?" the trail boss asked.

"Sure, Will, but I won't make an offer until tomorrow."

Whittle grinned.

The thunderheads now loomed so high that they formed a wall the color of a medicine bottle clear across the west, blanking out the sun. Freshets of chill air scurried along the ground, whipping dust. Lightning sheeted through the opaque sky.

If the skies opened up, he'd be stuck here. Those thin buggy tires would sink right into the prairie gumbo.

Whittle's foreman called a halt about nine miles south of town, in a dished hollow well east of the Chisholm. A slow spring would provide a little water; a deluge would provide the rest.

The broker and owner watched the restless cattle mill, sniff tired grass, or crowd around the spring. These hands could be chasing Bar W cattle halfway back to Texas if the storm set them off.

"You want to ride in for a closer look? I'll lend you a saddler," Whittle said.

"No, I've already seen what I want to see, Will."

What he had seen was wild stuff, rangy bulls, snorty cows, mean heifers, and assorted spooky yearlings. They were showing some famine in their rump and gut. Their age ranged wildly from eight or ten down to less than a year. Mostly tough beef, soup and stew meat.

"If they don't run tonight, the best I can do is fourteen, minus three for shipping and one for me. I pay the city for the pens, and my men ride with the beef. If they run tonight, I'll have to take another look tomorrow."

"Ten dollars!"

"It could be worse tomorrow," McCoy said pregnantly. "Tell you what. I'll shake hands on it, stampede or not. Fourteen a head any way you want it."

Will Whittle grumbled, stalked out on the prairie, spat down the wind, returned, and shook hands. Addison McCoy beat it out of there just as fast as his trotter could haul him north.

CHAPTER 10

Addison McCoy knew Hash Brown, after a
fashion. They had clashed at Pea Ridge, when
McCoy was a lieutenant under Sam Curtis.
Brown's company had fought bravely, wasting
itself on the entrenched Union Army.

Now Brown was coming. McCoy didn't know
how much credence to give to the legends.
Texans had a way of inflating things ten times
larger than life. But even if half true, Hash
Brown would be a man to reckon with.

McCoy raced toward Opportunity just ahead
of the storm, but didn't escape it. A mile south
of the river, the deluge caught him, the rain
roaring and hissing and smacking his face. The
terrified horse bolted toward the livery barn, ca-
reening across the slippery bridge and into
town, out of control. McCoy thought his deliv-
erance was miraculous.

An hour later, in warm and dry clothing, he
siphoned some Knoxville hundred-proof
whiskey into a tumbler in his room at the Stockmen's Hotel, added a splash, and sipped gingerly. The whiskey drove the last of his chill out
of him.

He had decisions to make, and some sipping

always quickened his mind. The Civil War had never quite ended in the Kansas cowtowns. The Texas drovers had either fought in the war or had older brothers or fathers who did. They had no use for Yanks.

The same was true of the Union men, who remembered Bloody Lawrence and were still avenging it. Jayhawkers, largely Union veterans gone sour, stalked the Texas trail herds, and the Texans sometimes tore a Kansas cowtown to pieces if they didn't like the treatment they were receiving.

Brown's previous drives to Abilene and Newton had been bloody and evoked horror. Legend had it that he always arrived with more cattle than he had when he started up the trail, and if he didn't like the price offered for them at the railroad yards, he threatened to tear the town apart. Word also had it that he buried bodies along the way.

Now he was on his way to Opportunity. And he would be peddling longhorns to his old nemesis from Pea Ridge.

The whiskey sipped just fine.

McCoy downed the last of it in a hurry, let it heat his belly for a moment, then stood and peered out the hotel window onto a wet street in which every puddle was silvered by the twilight sky. The rain had stopped.

He doffed his slippers and tugged his ancient corral-muck boots over his feet, ignoring the incongruity of the beslimed footwear and his tailored broadcloth suit and paisley cravat. He saved his good boots for clement weather.

He knew where to find Spade Ball.

The town marshal occupied his usual stand at the far end of the long mahogany bar in the Lone Star, the spot where shapely serving girls collected their drinks from the bartender and suffered a cheerful grope from the lawman.

That's where Ball kept an eye on the cowboys, looking for faint reasons, or no reason at all, to finger them. Marty Drum's only request was to nip the Texans out on the street; not in his emporium of delights and entertainments.

McCoy approached directly, feeling a little out of place in his sharp-creased suit.

He interrupted the marshal's banter with a sallow tinhorn and invited the man outside.

"Need to speak in confidence," he said.

Out in the fresh, chill air, with water still dripping from the eaves, he warned the marshal about the two outfits arriving in two or three weeks, both owned by Hash Brown.

"There'll be maybe thirty men, most of them veterans, and every one of them dangerous," he said. "You might consider taking measures."

"What measures?"

"You'll be grossly outnumbered by hard men. It would not be wise to provoke them unless you prefer a bloodbath. No jail can hold them, especially not yours."

A smile built on Ball's weathered face. "They can't come in here armed," he said. "I think provoking them Rebs might just be the thing to do. There's profit in it."

McCoy refrained from calling the man a fool. He also refrained from arguing further. One of his few gifts, he often told himself, was an insight into men.

"You're warned," he said and wheeled away.

Spade Ball chuckled.

They were all warned, the whole political crowd. Ball would swiftly inform the mayor, the city clerk, the councilmen, Judge Wannamaker, and a few merchants as well. Drum's ring. That's what a few astute men were quietly calling that crowd.

McCoy slopped his way back to Main Street. The dark bulk of the Merchant Bank of Opportunity stood on the corner. He thought of the gold and currency he kept in its vault.

He debated whether to go back to the hotel and dine, or whether to talk to Angie. His boots had sponged up muck, and clammy cold water slithered around his toes. Once he returned, he would take off the wet boots.

Angie, then.

He could see the lamplight in the window of *The Outlook*, half a block distant. The woman never slept. A paper that size usually employed three full-time people and one or two more part-time.

He felt the squish of the mire as he plowed up the mucky street, and then pushed open one of the glassed double doors. She wore her smock and was setting type under a green-shaded lamp over the composing stone.

"Addison!"

"You have a minute?"

"You have news?"

"I imagine."

"Then I'll stop." She carefully set down her type stick. "It's unending," she said.

He settled on a stool next to hers, hoping he wouldn't get ink on his suit. Swiftly he described his trip south to bid on Will Whittle's stock and told her about Hash Brown.

"I've heard of him. Everyone has," she said. "Let me see. You probably told Spade about it, and he laughed at you."

She was a good news hawk.

He smiled. "So I'm telling you. Looks like you have maybe two issues to clean up Opportunity. After that . . . there may not be any Opportunity."

"Did Spade even listen?"

"Guess."

She smiled. "How did you phrase it?"

"I said the town should do nothing to provoke that bunch. I'm thinking they wouldn't mind leveling Opportunity the way the Rebs burned Lawrence."

"Did you talk to Marty?"

"No, a word in Spade's ear will spread to the whole city hall gang. Ah, Drum's Ring."

She didn't react to the sobriquet. "I guess I'll write something about justice around here. I was planning to, anyway. I've tried to look at Sid Wannamaker's court records, but he manages to misplace them when I ask. I guess I'll say so . . ."

"And Marty?"

They had come to the crux of it.

"It's not easy to criticize your own son or his politics," she said, and then met his gaze resolutely. "But I will. There are things a good editor has to do. Gideon always talked about that, but it never came to roost until now.

"I can stand up for what's right, or not. I can go beyond family and blood ties and seek justice. That's what this is, you know. Injustice.

"Most of those boys up from Texas are just friendly galoots having a good time and doing nothing very rowdy except maybe drinking too much and . . ." she let the rest remain unspoken. "If there's a legitimate offense, disturbing the peace, I'm all for fining them.

"If it's just Marty's and Sid's and Spade's racket . . . so help me, Addison, I'll start a little campaign on my front page. That's my choice. Injustice is one of the worst evils to befall anyone. Even petty injustice."

McCoy thought maybe she was a woman he could fall for, but she had never encouraged any man.

"Not much time. Maybe reforming our marshal and the court won't do a bit of good. Man like Brown, he won't care one way or the other. He's a man born to trouble."

"But I can try. Thank you. You've heartened me. I was wavering . . . This is Monday. I print Wednesday night. There's time."

"I don't know how you manage."

"I don't," she said, and plucked up her type stick after brushing back a vagrant strand of graying hair.

He got the message and retreated into the dank, summer night. Main Street had turned into a morass and it sucked at his boots all the way back to the hotel, like a beggar trying to impede his progress.

The Stockmen's had laid a coarse old rug on the veranda next to a bootjack, and he took the hint. He left his down-at-the-heel veterans alongside a dozen other pairs and headed for the saloon.

He slid into a wooden booth, and there must have been something about his demeanor that kept others at bay because no one joined him. That was what he wanted. The barkeep brought him his usual Knoxville whiskey, and he sipped slowly.

Maybe it was time to leave Opportunity. Catch the next express west. He had always known the place would dry up and blow away when the herds stopped coming. New towns were springing up along with new trails like the Goodnight-Loving. And the Atchison, Topeka and Santa Fe was laying rail out there somewhere.

He'd been married once to an oatmeally

woman, pale as milk, soft as whipped cream, as wary of the empty sky as a prairie dog. They had tried to have a family, but after two miscarriages and a stillborn boy, they gave up. After the war he came home and didn't want a pudding wife and left her. Both families were scandalized. He never regretted the divorce.

He had been progressing toward California ever since. Kansas was no place for a civilized man, but the cowtowns offered rich rewards to a fair-dealing, shrewd businessman, and he had profited from them. Each Kansas town had been a stepping-stone into the West. There was enough in the vault at the Merchant Bank to do something big in California. He had intended to wait for the end of the shipping season before deciding whether it would be his last in Opportunity.

In California he would find the sort of woman he wanted; young, dark haired, olive-skinned, fiery, fierce, mysterious, exotic, unyielding, firm-fleshed, passionate, reckless, and tender. That would take time and money. He had both, and a working knowledge of Spanish as well.

He sipped and decided not to quit Opportunity just yet. If Angie could brave the storm, he could, too.

CHAPTER 11

Angie was too busy summing up a delinquent advertising account to notice the cowboy at first. But when she did look up, she beheld a thin Texan standing calmly at the counter. At once she detected something different about him and it proved to be gold-rimmed spectacles. She had never seen a cowboy wearing those.

"Are you the editor, ma'am?"

"Cook and bottle washer, too."

"Have you a moment?"

"Have you news?"

"Well, not exactly —"

"Then I'm afraid —"

"Five minutes?"

She waved him past the counter to a battered chair next to hers.

"What?" she asked.

"I'm Richard Baylor, ma'am. With Will Whittle's outfit. We're holding cattle three miles out, waiting for stock cars."

She waited, ready to cut him off.

"I'm sorry to take your time. I guess maybe I'll go . . ."

"Something brought you here."

"Justice."

She settled back in her swivel chair. "Take all the time you want, Mr. Baylor."

"Mr. Whittle let half of us go to town last night. Tonight the other half can come in. He gave us our trail wage — three months, ninety dollars. Most of us buy new outfits first. I did," he said, pointing to stiff jeans and a new shirt. "The old stuff, it's worth a bonfire. And we all get barbered and bathed and cleaned up. That's before anything else, for most of us anyway."

She sensed what was coming.

"We went on over to the Lone Star to wet our whistles. None of us have seen a drop in three months, and we'd built up a thirst.

"I'm a little different. One or two beers are fine with me. I was planning on a good sit-down restaurant dinner, in a real chair, with some real greens and all . . . only I never got there."

She sighed. "The marshal?"

"I stepped outside onto that plank walk, stretched a bit, and next I knew this big marshal lays a hand on me and says I'm disturbing the peace. And off we go. I was no more disturbing the peace last night than I am now. I wasn't violating any law. I wasn't wearing a sidearm. I wasn't drunk, and I wasn't a vagrant.

"So I asked him how come, and he says it's obvious to him I'm trouble. Well, when we got to the jailhouse I found half a dozen other Texians locked in there, and they rounded us all up and marched us across the street to the justice of the peace, and he read us the charges. He said we could post bail for twenty dollars and forfeit it and walk out, or we could go to trial in two weeks."

She sensed a great earnestness in this man. He seemed more serious, more mature, than the usual Texas hell-raisers.

"They all paid, everyone but me. I value my money. That fine was almost equal to a month's wage. So I said I'd go to trial, and I didn't mind sitting in their pokey because I have a book, and I like to read.

"Then that justice got mad at me and said I'd cost the city lots of meals. I just told him that was fine; I'd wait, and he and the marshal fumed and fussed and finally hauled me back to the jail — the rest of the Texians were gone by then — and they threw me in. I just got out an hour ago. Ma'am, that constable took every cent out of my jeans and tossed me into the street this morning. I had about forty-eight dollars left after outfitting, and he took it. Twenty for the justice court and the rest for him, he said. So that's why I'm here. Justice."

She stared out the front doors into a sunlit street that was whited with mock virtue. The muck had mostly dried under the ruthless Kansas sun. Somehow, she knew this moment would come, and she knew its meaning to her, and she knew its consequences. She knew that she would cross a bridge, her Rubicon, and her life would change. She knew she might end up in another trade. Or worse.

But she didn't matter much. Justice did.

"I would like to do a story about that, Mr. Baylor."

"I was hoping you would."

"You are well spoken."

"I went to a normal school for a year. I wanted to be a teacher. But I wanted to live outdoors even more. Will Whittle's the same way. He's got rivers of wisdom flowing through him, but he likes sunshine, and the sight of a thousand beeves trailing along, fat and strong."

She reached for her notepad and the stubby pencil and wrote a few words that would jog her memory when she did the story. With a few more questions she obtained his age and history and a solid understanding of just what had transpired the previous night.

"What book did you plan to read for two weeks in our jail, Mr. Baylor?"

"A law text, ma'am, Blackstone's *Commentaries*. I'm thinking I'll take it up some day, after a few more years of this."

"We could use a lawyer here, Mr. Baylor. But we're not a county seat. At least not yet."

"Yes, you could use a lawyer," he said. "He'd have his hands full all summer."

"Year around," she replied.

"I'm curious, Mrs. Drum. I understand you're the mayor's mother."

"Yes."

"Am I barking up the wrong tree?"

"Up until a few days ago you would have

been, I'm ashamed to say."

He smiled slightly. This cerebral man wasn't the usual sort of cowboy. "Then perhaps my story will see daylight."

"On the front page, with a headline of the largest display type I have."

"May I ask what has changed your mind?"

"Justice, Mr. Baylor."

"Will there be consequences?"

"I'm prepared to endure them."

His face wreathed into delight. "I'll stick around just to see it."

He stood. She shook his hand and watched the lean man drop a weathered hat over his red hair and exit into that sunlight.

She watched him go.

Everything was different.

She donned her printer's apron and began setting the story at once, composing it as she plucked letters from the upper and lower caseboxes. Her fingers acted unruly, and her hands sweated, and she knew the story would be shot with typos. Fear feathered through her, and nothing would erase it.

The story kept growing. The more she set of it, inch after column inch, the more it mushroomed. She had known a great deal; Baylor's story would merely be the news peg for a longer examination of the abuse of the justice system.

She had plenty to report, including the virtual absence of records. Most of those Texans who had been skinned in Spade Ball's iron-strap shakedown parlor had never even been recorded on the big gray ledger at his desk. Others appeared merely as a name, without a date or indication of the offense. And as for Sid Wannamaker, she hadn't been given access to his court records for weeks. They should have been available for public examination.

Eventually her story grew too long, and she broke it into pieces: the main story would recount the bookish Richard Baylor's ordeal and loss. A sidebar would focus on the city marshal's methods of fattening his wallet and perhaps the wallets of others. Another would discuss drumhead justice in Sid Wannamaker's court. Another would examine the whole structure of licensing fees for saloons, gambling tables, billiard halls, variety theaters, and other dubious fleshpots down there in Texas Town, as some people called it.

She worked steadily the entire day, and by late afternoon she carried the heavy galley trays over to the proofing bench, ran an ink-charged sponge over the type, laid a proof sheet over the type, and ran an impression.

In spite of the blurry type and sticky black ink, the story leapt up at her, puissant and penetrating. It shook her. This story would be the harkening of change in Opportunity. It would be the ruin of small empires . . . including her son's.

She marked the typos, reset, and ran another proof. She wanted this story to be perfect. This time she corrected three more typos and re-wrote a few lines that seemed vague. If she was going to turn Opportunity upside down and throw light on conduct that would overturn the city administration, her story had better be concise, accurate, and complete.

She wrestled with that, avoiding the fearsome implications of what she was doing. She found comfort in small things, figures of speech, grammar, perfecting a good lead; everything that she had learned on her own and that Gideon had taught her.

The sun hung low before she completed work on the big story, and she had yet to make up the pages, correct some ads, set some minor stories, and proof the four pages, one by one. Fortunately, the news hole was smaller than normal. At the height of the shipping season merchants were touting anything that might attract the Texas dollar.

She wondered what sort of news hole she would have the following week — if any.

She wasn't ready to begin the presswork until ten, and knew that she would be lucky to finish by midnight. Wearily, wishing once again she could find someone to help her, she began cranking the sheets through the unforgiving Washington press, one by one, side by side, the operation she dreaded the most. But eventually the finished *Outlook*s were stacked and drying, ready for folding and delivery in the morning.

She poured some water into the basin and

scrubbed. She felt particularly alone in that deep-night moment, in the light of one coal oil lamp. But she felt Gideon's presence — not as a ghost — but as a guardian spirit.

Tomorrow she would do things just as she always had: fold the papers, give them to her two newsboys, Jackie and Aubrey, and then haul the rest to the post office where old Horatio Bates would send them winging.

She turned down the lamp until the wick blued out. Bed looked especially inviting that night. But she was elated.

CHAPTER 12

Smiling Marty Drum, mayor of Opportunity, wasn't smiling much that day. Angie and her paper had elected him, and now Angie and her paper were busily unelecting him.

At least, he figured, that's what his mother thought. Marty had different plans. No one had awakened him. Here, on the pages of *The Outlook*, a genuine earthquake was shaking Opportunity, but no one had rattled his doorknob, and he had slept blissfully into the hot morning.

Now, mid-afternoon, Marty Drum's ring had assembled in his upstairs quarters to sweat, curse the damp heat, and maybe curse Marty's ma. Present at this hastily called conference were his city clerk, Dinky Smothers, the two city aldermen Mo Baskin and Arnold Marlowe, Spade Ball and Eddie Farrar from the marshal's office, and half a dozen others, all closely tied to Marty's little green machine.

They all oozed sweat. The breezes had perversely quit, and rank bodies were rendering the parlor unbearable.

"I know something about newspapers. We can lick this if you'll do exactly as I say," Marty said.

The assorted gents, oozing malice as well as sweat, simply stared.

"First of all, don't threaten her. She'll print it. A few threats are exactly what she wants. Got that?"

He glared at the sullen city marshal, who glared back.

"Spade, dammit, don't do it. You try wrecking her plant and all she'll do is print the next paper in Hutchinson or Abilene, and bleat about your bad habits right on page one. You'd have to wreck every printing plant in a hundred-mile radius to stop *The Outlook*."

"I'll sue for libel," Ball growled.

Marty bore down. "Winning a libel suit requires two things: you must prove that the defamatory material was false, and you have to prove malice, which is defined as a willful and reckless disregard for truth.

"A simple mistake is usually not libelous, especially if the error is retracted. Truth is a valid defense in libel, no matter how badly someone's reputation suffers. So, sue her up in Abilene. See how far you get."

The marshal retreated into his sweat.

Marty felt his own face drip and knew his shirt had plastered itself to his chest.

"What we're going to do is clam up, every one of us, until it blows over. She'll grow tired of the game after a few issues if no one responds, and life in Opportunity will proceed exactly as before.

"Remember, it's a year until the city elections of 1878, and by that time the whole issue will be dead. Don't ever suppose a voter has even a one-month memory. Remember also, there are only a hundred-seventy registered voters in town, and we have a hundred-twenty-five of them in our pocket. Almost every property owner in town. Who the hell wants to pay taxes?"

"Maybe we can make a show of changing things," said Councilman Marlowe. "The least we can do is go easy on the cowboys. Just let 'em go, Sid. Don't be so rough."

Judge Wannamaker glared. "Are you suggesting my court isn't up to your standards? I do what's necessary for public safety. Those cowboys are animals, and if I go soft, they'll threaten the peace and safety of this town. Not to mention its women. I should fine you, too, Marlowe."

"The hell with that," Marty said. "We need the money. That's our salaries, our law enforcement, our building and maintenance fund, our volunteer fire department, and all the rest."

Billy de Vere, the stableman, supplied one of his ready-made quips. "Just don't pick on no Texans with spectacles," he said.

But no one laughed.

"How about you talk to your mother?" asked Spade Ball. "You're the big potato here, so get to work on it. You good for some arm-twisting or are you a mama's boy?"

Marty sighed. "She's got the bit in her mouth, and I can't turn her now. Just do what I say, clam up, and she'll figure it out. And, oh, yeah, there is one thing. Don't advertise. I'm talking to you, Billy. And you can pass word to the rest. From now on, any merchant who runs an ad in that paper, I figure he's working against the elected mayor and the administration."

"Will that stop her?"

Marty grinned. "Sure," he said. Actually, it would just stir his ma into fighting form, but at least she'd get the message that no responsible person agreed with her.

Mo Baskin, who'd been silent, suddenly stood and stared at the town marshal. "You've been cleaning out the pockets of those cowboys and fattening your own purse and not sharing it. That damned well should stop. It's one thing to fine those Texans for getting out of hand, but this other . . ."

Ball glared. "You watch out, Mo."

"Spade, lay off him," Marty said. "And watch yourself."

The city marshal glowered.

"I don't like this bloody blight," Sid Wannamaker said. "If we keep quiet and she keeps hammering, pretty soon the state's going to have a look. My justice court's under the supervision of superior courts, and all I see is woe and grief. No, Marty, I don't think I'll clam up at all. If your little old ma picks on me, I'll tell her that I'm preserving the public safety around

100

here, and she can put that in her pipe and smoke it."

Marty nipped a Havana, scratched a lucifer and ignited it, and puffed, mostly to give himself time to think. He had a roomful of sweating apes threatening to tear apart his machine.

"Sid, give my plan a chance. Give me six more weeks. The shipping season will be over, even the last tag end of it, and Angie's fire-eating crusade will grind into dust when there's no cowboys in sight. You start arguing with her, and you'll just feed the fire."

Ball stood. "It's hot in here; I'm going," said the marshal.

He and his deputy stalked out, clomping down those wooden stairs, leaving the rest of them dripping in silence.

"You should fire him," Mo Baskin said. "He's giving the town a black eye."

"Why? He earns every cent. He's a brave man, and he keeps a lid on this town. Every day he wades into those wild Texans, some of them armed in spite of the ordinance, and keeps order. You know what would happen without Spade Ball or someone like him? Nothing would be safe. No person, no life, no property, no horse."

"He's violating state law."

"You should be grateful he's around, Mo."

"It's hot. I'm going."

They all trooped out.

Marty wished for a breeze, anything to

cleanse his rooms of the odor. He decided to get out, too. He couldn't stand to be inside one more minute.

He found himself drifting, against his own will, toward the paper. Well, he was different. He could talk. She was his ma. So he trudged along Kansas Street, sticking to the shady side such as it was, and turned in at the big double doors. His mother was breaking down the new edition, her damp hair clinging to her face, and her forehead wet with sweat.

"I've been expecting you," she said.

"Can we talk?"

"Everything you say gets quoted."

"Can we talk just family-like, you and me?"

"Sure, and it all gets quoted."

He laughed, or made a sweaty effort at it. "What are you doing it for?"

"Justice."

"Going against me?"

"Seeing that justice is done."

"The advertising's going to dry up."

"I knew it would come to that."

"Then why write this?"

"Because it's right."

He discovered tears welling from her dark eyes and mixing with the beads of sweat on her face.

The sight of her weeping fixated him, and he could not turn aside. There she was, his mother, in pain, and he had started those tears.

"I'm sorry," he said.

She shook her head violently. "Go away, Marty. Don't come back until you do the right thing," she said.

He sighed. The air in the shop oppressed him. She was melting old typemetal in the furnace, which made the whole room unbearable.

There wasn't anything more to say to her, so he left, descending the single step to the board-walk and better air. But he carried the oppression of that room with him and didn't like the feeling.

He was angry.

The break was her fault; not his. What had he done? She had started it. He fumed his way back to the saloon, wanting an ice-cold drink, but there wasn't a sliver of ice anywhere in Opportunity. Joe Sawyer's pond ice, carefully packed in sawdust last winter, had run out the week before and now the Lone Star dished out tepid whiskey and warm beer in a blazing June sun.

She was missing him much more than he was missing her, he thought. She had always fussed over him. Her dreams for him were more ambitious than his own, and she had fostered his political ambitions in her paper. He was her only flesh and blood, and now she'd cut the cord. It must have been hard, making that choice. But she did, and now they were free of each other. In a way.

Maybe that was good. He didn't need her at all, and sometimes wished she would move away. It wasn't that he didn't care; it was that her presence, and her newspaper, were a restraint, like some cyclops eye staring at the whole town, an eye without lids that never stopped seeing.

Well, what did it matter? He had the best resort in town, and it was coining money every shipping season. He was a public official, the mayor, and his word was law in Opportunity. He had a safe bulging with gold and greenbacks.

He had his choice of women. At least women of a certain type. The one who really interested him, Melanie Garrity, the banker's daughter, was beyond his reach and betrothed anyway. The only cloud, and it was coming closer each year, was the end of the trail drives. But when that happened, he'd move his club west. And leave Opportunity to his ma.

Funny how she was crying like that.

CHAPTER 13

The silent treatment. Angie smiled. That was Marty's finagling. He had been around newspapers enough to know a few things, like when to shut up. If it weren't for Marty, Spade Ball would be snorting like a picadored bull, and Sid Wannamaker would be eviscerating her for contempt of court, and the aldermen would be tubthumping some ordinances to license and tax newspapers.

She took the silence as a good omen. They knew full well that if they bleated, they would see their caterwauling on the front page. Still, she itched to know what the rest of the town thought, if anything. She had grasped one verity early in life, and journalism had taught it to her: most people didn't care about anything other than their own lives.

She discovered, when she looked up from her accounting, the portly presence of the postmaster, Horatio Bates, peering nosily at her ledgers.

"Why, Horatio, what on earth —"

"I've closed shop for ten minutes. Out to lunch, it says. The train is late anyway." He leaned toward her. "Any result?"

"Oh, you mean from the story about corruption?"

He nodded.

"Nothing, Horatio, not a blooming thing. None of the suspects has made an appearance, my wayward son avoids the maternal presence, and no upright citizen has walked in to garland me."

He laughed. "I commend you. You've done a brave thing, and I want you to know it. I did hear a few whispers this morning. People talk as if I'm not present behind the counter, which gives them leave to wag their tongues. Mostly, it's wait-and-see. They're not sure they want fire-eating newspaper crusades in Opportunity, especially about tax reform, which could pinch their purses."

"Well, neither am I. Especially one that hurts Marty."

Bates gazed at her kindly. "That's what makes you so unusual, Angie. Not one in a thousand mothers would set blood ties aside for something larger."

She felt her spirits crumpling. "I haven't set anything aside. Marty's my boy," she replied. She tried hard to hide from his gentle scrutiny, but knew she was transparent to him.

"You know, you're as glittering as goldmine shares," he said.

"I've never been compared to a stock certificate," she replied, tartly.

"Angie, take heart. That's all I'm here to say.

You're a true blessing to this town, and I'm honored to know you." His gaze was so gentle and warm that she melted.

"Oh, Horatio. . . ." She swallowed back the tears and smiled.

"I have to go peddle stamps and console widows. Oh, yes, some dowager new in our precincts, a Mrs. Busby, inquired about employment. I suggested she come see you."

"What can she do?"

"You'll have to ask her that. I know only that you're overworked."

With that, the postmaster took his stately leave. She always wished she could help him exit. Departing required large social skills, which few had mastered, especially Horatio. He always turned windbaggy about the time he was fixing to leave.

Well, damn the entire population of Opportunity. She had exposed the venality of public officials beyond a shadow of doubt, and not one upright citizen had cheered, endorsed, hugged, or otherwise celebrated her work, except the postmaster.

She gathered her advertising statements, her proof copies and her order pad, and headed into the clay streets. Display advertising was the lifeblood of a newspaper, and she solicited it even before she wrote the first story for the next issue.

She flipped her window sign to CLOSED and departed into a pleasant morning, with puffball

107

clouds scudding past. A cool breeze freshened Opportunity.

As always, she started at Leif Torvold's tan-brick bakery, and found flour-dusted Marguerite Torvold within.

"Here's your proof copy and your statement. How about next week? The usual? Want to feature something?"

Marguerite pursed up a smile. "I'll ask," she said, wiping her rosy fingers on a starchy apron. She vanished into the rear, releasing a bloom of yeasty air that instantly reduced Angie to starvation.

Moments later Mrs. Torvold returned. "The same, yes, and we're going to feature sugared doughnuts next week."

"Two columns by eight, sugared doughnuts. All right, I'll send you the ad when it's done."

That had gone well.

But at Al Bannister's cigar store, she ran into trouble.

"Yeah, this time I'll pay, but no more, not until you get off your high horse, picking on the constables like that."

"Sorry, Al. Hate to lose your support. You've been a good account, and I think your ads have brought in some business for you. But I'm going to keep on writing about them until there's justice in Opportunity."

"Trouble, that's all it is. You should get married."

She laughed. How many times had she heard

that? Every time someone didn't like something she published, she was advised to get married. Wedlock, they believed, would cool down her hot flashes.

It turned out to be a mixed morning. Some merchants, like Ed Wilber, supported her and even bought a larger ad. Others, like the reptilian liveryman Billy de Vere lashed into her, told her to get the hell out and not come back, and tore up her invoice in front of her eyes. She decided he was nothing but a petty crook.

"Billy, you've been around horse apples too long," she said.

"Out!" he bellowed.

Some merchants and the bankers thought her crusade was farsighted and valuable. Some didn't like it but bought ads anyway because they needed to hawk their wares.

By the time she'd made her rounds, she knew she had lost some display advertising, maybe a quarter of it, but it could have been worse. *The Outlook* wasn't going to starve to death, at least as long as the fence-sitters straddled the fence.

Maybe that was just fine. She would have a bigger news hole just when she had plenty to say.

A generously rounded woman in a flowered blue chapeau and a prim dress sat on the bench in front of the newspaper.

"You're Mrs. Busby. Please come in." Angie pushed open the unlocked door and set her order pad on the desk.

"Gladys Busby. Call me Aunt Gladys."

"You must be someone's auntie."

"I wish to be everyone's aunt, lacking children of my own."

"Mr. Bates said you were looking for employment. What do you do?"

"I write sermons."

"Ah . . . sermons?"

"Yes, for my late husband, the Reverend Mr. Desmond Busby."

"Not here."

"Kansas City. I pined for a new life and bought a ticket to Opportunity. I am at Mrs. Hoffmeister's female boarding residence, which is entirely respectable and examined weekly for cockroaches."

"Ah, what else do you do?"

"Just sermons. You have a great need for sermons, madam. I have no doubt of it. I have ears. You're being whacked right and left, with staves and switches and whips. You should hear what's being said at Mrs. Hoffmeister's table. It just happens that I am proficient at sermons."

"How would writing sermons help me?"

"With rebuke, Mrs. Drum. We shall smite the moneychangers on hip and thigh, drive them out of the temple with a whip."

"Ah, I'm afraid that isn't what I need. Sorry."

"Then I shall work for nothing."

"Mrs. Busby —"

"Aunt Gladys."

"Well, Aunt Gladys, if you were a compositor

or a pressman or an advertising salesman or an accountant . . ."

"I did the books."

"The church ledgers?"

"And ours. The reverend's and mine. And who's better at getting subscriptions and advertising than a preacher's wife?"

"I wouldn't know."

"That's all right. You probably haven't been inside a church for years. I can tell. You aren't ungodly, but do want some schooling. Now, where do I hang my coat?"

"If you work here, you will get ink over everything you wear."

"That's quite all right; I shall consider it something holy, like communion wine."

Angie showed the woman the plant, emphasizing the amount of black ink that would be transferred from every surface to Mrs. Busby's fingers, face, skirts, cuffs, and stockings.

It was worth a try. Maybe Gladys would be heaven-sent relief for a woman who hated bookkeeping. Angie would rather stomp the perverse press than keep her ledgers.

"Very well, Aunt Gladys. Here are the ledgers. There's a stack of invoices. Here's a stack of receipts."

Aunt Gladys settled her rotund self into the protesting chair, lifted a gold pince-nez to her coy white nose, examined Angie's handiwork with her doe's eyes, and harrumped.

Angie stared.

Aunt Gladys sorted through bills and receipts harrumping and mumbling.

"Is something wrong?"

The woman peered at Angie over her pince-nez and clucked.

"Well, I'm going to build the ads," Angie said, feeling miffed. If the woman didn't like her bookkeeping, she could go keep books at the bank.

The woman pursed her beestung lips.

"I pay help a dollar a day," Angie said, irritation building in her.

"I don't know how you can afford it," Aunt Gladys said. "You don't charge enough for your ads. When I make up next week's invoices, I'll hike the price fifty percent."

"No, don't! I'm charging all that the traffic will bear. I know exactly what these merchants are willing to pay."

Aunt Gladys smiled benevolently. "Don't let them fool you," she said. "The ones who slither a button into the collection plate were always the richest. Desmond always left it to me to make the necessary pastoral call, and once we had our little visit, the buttons vanished."

"And so did your parishioners."

"Oh, tut. You go prepare your advertising, the crasser the better, and I'll do the ledger, and then I'll write the sermon."

"I don't wish to have a sermon."

"Oh, it's a figure of speech. What's lacking is a

logical, purposeful, unassailable editorial in each issue. Opinion. Leadership. Angie, my dear, we shall throw the rascals out."

CHAPTER 14

Marty Drum knew full well that neither official silence nor loss of advertising would slow down his determined mother. Now that she had an assistant she would simply devote even more time to her crusade. It didn't annoy him; he rather enjoyed her feistiness. But of course, he could not permit that yellow-dog paper to flummox the ring.

The Honorable Drum was not without resources. Over the next days, he wired classified ads and employment offers to various compass points, but mostly to burgs located along the railroad tracks as far east as St. Louis. These were directed to the local printing shops and papers. He wished to hire a compositor and printer for his family-owned paper and would offer such emoluments as to attract a gifted and experienced journeyman. That may have been a little vague, but enough to entice various candidates to hop the next coach — or boxcar — to Opportunity and consult with him.

He knew he wouldn't wait long for a few printers to trickle in, mostly of the tramp variety, which was exactly what Marty had in mind. These sots of the open road drifted from paper to paper, lingering long enough to set a few thousand ems, get some plunder for whiskey, then meander down the lonesome trail once again, their employment as temporary as their loyalties.

The West brimmed with tramp printers, nearly all of them well acquainted with a bottle. Within two days, Marty found himself interviewing the first of these Knights of the Upper Case and rejecting the man as too supine, if not obsequious. Marty wanted a two-hundred pounder, impervious to female fists and wiles and oblivious to all authority but Marty's own.

The third of these whiskey printers meandered in, having discovered the opening while talking to his journalistic colleagues in Wichita. Marty was conducting his interviews in the Lone Star Saloon, preferably afternoons. A Mr. Fox Purser, veteran of the ink pots, let it be known to the barkeep that he was available for interview and private treaty.

Thus did Marty descend the stairs to the emporium and discover a brute of a man, bullet-headed, thick-necked, and built along the lines of an inverted pyramid.

"At your service, Captain," said Purser. "I hear you want a man for your little weekly."

"I do. A reliable, skilled, able man to set type, do the pages, and run a Washington acorn press."

"With my eyes closed I do such things. But what's the hitch? Why are you offering a wanderer more than the usual sixty cents for a thousand ems?"

Marty smiled. "How about a drink, Mr. Purser?"

"I never pass an opportunity to comfort my heart and soul, Mr. Drum."

Marty ordered a double Paducah, and, in short order, the amber nectar was laid before the vagrant compositor.

"Now you see, my mother's the editor, but of course this is the family paper, and we're having a little tussle . . ."

"Ah, blessed be thy name," said Purser, sipping. The printer's face reposed in angelic serenity.

Marty did not know whether the doxology was in honor of the good whiskey or the conditions of employment. He concluded that Fox Purser was not an unsophisticated gent, and therefore some illumination about what might be required had been processed within his cranium.

He swiftly laid it out: *The Outlook* might be nominally his mother's, but Purser would work entirely for Marty, and be paid by Marty, and do exactly what Marty required.

"Ah . . . ," said Purser with deepening enthusiasm.

"I'll pay the usual, plus free drinks and meals here, plus certain bonuses when certain results have been achieved."

"Ah . . ."

Cheerfully, for this was proceeding just as he had hoped, Marty described what he wanted. His mother was on the warpath; she threatened the mayor's administration as well as the town's finance and other less public wallets.

"Your task, Mr. Purser, is to keep all such material out of the paper. Your methods may be whatever you choose short of bodily harm. You may be absentminded, you may pie the type, you may doctor the copy, whatever suits you. Your zeal must match hers, and your wiles must outfox hers, if I may permit myself a bon mot."

"Ah . . . ah . . ." Purser rolled it around on his tongue like a good Havana. "But what if your mother fires me?"

"Ignore her."

"What if she gets the constable to throw me out the door?"

"I assure you, my town marshal will listen politely and do nothing."

Purser sighed. "I shall feel like a rat."

"That's because you are one. You settled that question by accepting my offer."

Purser smiled broadly. "Very well then, Mr. Mayor. You may pay me an advance of five cartwheels and I shall enthuse myself this evening at this establishment and report for work in the morning. But, ah . . . you will also have to put me up. I want fancy digs."

"That's easy, Mr. Purser. I keep a closet right here, with its own door opening on the alley, a small and odorous cubicle sometimes rented to whores and hop fiends, and since you qualify on all counts it will be yours for the duration. Consider the alley your outhouse."

Fox Purser licked his lips. "We have arrived at a sublime understanding," he said. "My type stick is at your command."

"So is your brain."

"Such as it is, Mr. Drum. It needs regular spiriting and tobaccoing to function in top form."

"She prints tomorrow. She's been talking to cowboys about their grievances and plans a new and arctic blast at the town coppers. You'll have to do a deal of sabotage on your very first day."

"A trifle, Mr. Drum, a mere trifle."

And in that manner the alliance was forged.

Marty hated to do it. He loved his ma, at least on weekends.

That settled, he dropped his straw Panama over his curly locks to stave off the barbarous sun, and hustled up to Kansas Street and the offices of *The Outlook*, where his mother would, even at that moment, be engaged in the demolition of his administration. He felt full of himself, joyous at the prospect of helping his mother put *The Outlook* out, thus alleviating her weariness, and at the same time controlling what went onto its pages. He expected the whiskey printer to vamoose in a month or so, and that would be just fine. By then the shipping season would be over, and she would have sewing bees and darning eggs in her columns.

Upon entering he discovered the new shrew, a veritable poulter, totting up the accounts while his beloved mother toiled at the composing bench; en flagrante delicto.

"Mother dear," he said.

"Marty," she said. She smiled and kept on slinging type. He was used to that. She never ceased to labor.

He beamed. "Luck is upon us. I've found a whiskey printer who'll work awhile."

"Who?" she asked.

"Fox Purser, one of the meandering breed, but probably worth a month's work and a good rest for you. I've hired him at my own expense to spare you any more burden. I've been wanting to do something for you. You look so tired, and I've felt guilty not helping you out."

This time she paused. "And what did you tell him?"

"That you're shorthanded. That you don't like wrestling the Washington press. That you need time to collect the news."

"And that I'm seeking certain reforms that you resist?"

"Oh, I gave him a vague idea, just to let him know how things are. But he'll be a fine addition to your staff, and frankly, I'm proud of myself. Your old Marty's looking after you. High time, eh?" He chuckled amiably.

"Marty, whenever you smile like that, I know I'm about to be swindled out of something."

"Well, you just see. He'll be here in the

morning to build the pages and do the press run. He's the lord of all presses and especially Hoe's Washington variety. What a relief, eh?"

"Maybe," she said, her gaze fastened to him like flypaper.

"Expect him before noon. He'll be entirely habeas corpus, but probably less than cognito before then. You know how they are."

She smiled. "Very well, Marty. Thank you for thinking of me. How often you are a blessing."

The tender and sorrowing look she offered him shot a tsunami of melancholia through him.

He preferred the hot sun.

Mayor Drum set his compass on the jail and sallied down the shady side of Kansas Street, past whitewashed emporiums that sold dry goods, boots and shoes, hats, ironware, furniture, hardware, ranching supplies, harness, apothecary goods, stationery, lumber, kerosene lamps, Havanas, ardent spirits, and ten-cent haircuts.

He turned at last into the fieldstone edifice where Spade Ball and his minions forted up, especially in the heat of the day. They were all night birds.

Spade was snoring on the hard single bunk of the cell. Mayor Drum clanged the barred door shut, grinning broadly. The clamor aroused the marshal.

"Shall I let you out?" he asked.

Ball puckered and spat and elaborately hoisted his holster around.

Mayor Drum opened the cell door, chortling.

"Tomorrow, my sainted mother will probably summon you to request that you evict a new employee at the paper," he said.

"I'll do it."

"No, you won't. I hired a printer, a drifter named Purser, to look after our affairs," Drum said.

"Ah," replied Ball, his eyebrows arching.

"He lives in my back room," Drum said. "He's on city salary. A public employee."

"Don't that beat all," the marshal said.

CHAPTER 15

Angie Drum eyed the new man warily. Unlike most runty knights of the road who drifted into her shop, this one was a big galoot. At the moment he was toiling with the type stick, setting the big story she had been working on all week.

His rheumy eyes and vein-shot proboscis told her much about him. Like the rest of his breed, he was indentured to spirits and would never escape. He would work in fits, with occasional disappearances, until he drifted on to another town. Most were temperamental and soon whined and grumbled themselves into quitting, usually a half hour before deadline.

But for the moment, he was gainfully employed. He had proved to be elaborately polite, courteous, even courtly, and seemed to possess an uncommon grip on the mother tongue. What's more, he was instantly at home and knew exactly what needed doing.

Maybe, just maybe, Marty's uncharacteristic gallantry was an act of kindness toward her, and not just another dodge. She toyed with the idea that Marty was a repentant son seeking the solace of maternal love, but the idea curdled the moment she stirred that pot.

Two employees at once. The idea dizzied her. As soon as Aunt Gladys had demonstrated some skills, Angie had taken time off to pursue the story she had planned for this issue. She had intended to drive out to the camps where cowboys were holding the herds until they could be shipped and talk to a few. In the past, she had always rented a buggy and quiet mare from Billy de Vere, but when she tried to rent the rig this time, he balked and turned surly.

So she wouldn't be leaving town anytime soon. Still, maybe that had become a blessing. The Texans she really wanted to talk to were those leaving town in the morning after spending a night enjoying Spade Ball's hospitality and visiting Justice of the Peace Sid Wannamaker's friendly tax office.

With her accountant holding the fort, she had grabbed a parasol and a notepad and ventured down to the bridge over the Arkansas, where all traffic into Opportunity was funneled. There, indeed, she had plenty of chances to talk to the Texas cowboys. She had only to ask a pointed question or two as they rode or trudged by, and soon had another anecdote, more resentment, another miscarriage of justice, to include in her growing catalogue of injustice and corruption.

She had intended to set the story herself this very morning, but found herself with a compositor dutifully plucking up letters and manufacturing lines of type. That was good enough for her. She sat down and penned her chronicle of

123

woe, taking each sheet back to Mr. Purser to set. Handwriting the story, scratching out words and revamping sentences until it shone, was a luxury she hadn't experienced since the days when she and Gideon had worked together.

With each page, Mr. Purser smiled and nodded and kept at his labor. The column of type in the galley tray stretched longer and longer; a foot, fifteen inches, twenty-four, and still she had not exhausted her notes.

For once she would reach press time without sliding into panic, and maybe they all could put the paper to bed during ordinary business hours.

All pages but the first had been completed, and now rested in their chases, ready to slide onto the flat bed of the press. The reform story would occupy most of the first page, along with cattle shipping news and the usual humor piece down in the lefthand corner.

Then Aunt Gladys appeared at her desk with an editorial in hand. "Read this," she said. "Smite them fore and aft."

"I think you are mixing your metaphors, Gladys," Angie said.

"I knew you would pick on me. My late husband was never satisfied with my work, even though he appropriated it for his own use. I was a dutiful wife, and now I shall be a dutiful employee and complaint shall never issue from my lips."

Angie laughed.

The opinion piece, penned in Gladys Busby's

fulsome hand, surprised Angie, though she couldn't quite say why. Maybe because she had expected a shrill and moralizing tone.

THE OUTLOOK has, for several weeks, been running accounts of petty graft and abuse of the judicial powers in Opportunity as a means to finance city government and dodge taxes.

It is not our intent to point fingers or make accusations here. The evidence is obvious and unimpeachable.

Instead, we wish to appeal to the conscience of the citizens of this town. We wish to appeal to your better natures, your sense of rightness and fitness. We wish to appeal to your unique and American understanding of what makes a good commonwealth and especially a small commonwealth such as the railroad shipping town of Opportunity.

It is time for change. The administration of justice is one of the most important functions of government. That, and keeping order, so that we may go about our business in safety, are the two main reasons governments are constituted and given authority over citizens.

In Opportunity, justice is being gravely traduced by venal interests and ambitions . . .

Angie thought it was a good editorial, sober, intelligent, and clearly an appeal to those transcending virtues that kept mortals from becoming predators.

"Gladys, this is a gem. You've expressed my very thoughts and done so graciously. Would you like to sign the editorial?"

"Only if you wish. I'd rather it simply be the viewpoint of the paper, Mrs. Drum."

Angie liked that, too.

"I'll have the new man set it," she said.

She carried the copy back to Mr. Purser. "We'll have a front-page editorial," she said. "When you're done with my story, set this, and that should be all we'll need. Maybe we can put it to bed early, for a change."

The compositor nodded benignly and continued his typesetting.

"This press has its quirks, so I'll help you do the run," she said. "We normally print about two hundred seventy, but I'm going to increase the run. We'll do three hundred this time."

By dinnertime the compositor had most of the story set.

"You run off and get something to eat, Mr. Purser. I'll proof this," she said.

The printer nodded, doffed his smock, and paused at the door. "I'll have me some soup and be right back, my lady."

He vanished.

"My lady indeed!" she exclaimed. She ran proofs of the story and found that he had composed the lines well, with few errors. There were only a few more inches to set, so she plucked up the type stick and went to work. By the time he returned, around eight, she had finished the story and was proofing it.

"You're a good compositor, Mr. Purser," she said. "Only seven typos. Here are the corrections. I'll start building the front page while you set the editorial. Set it ten point, two columns, and leave two ems on either side so we can box it."

He donned his stained smock again and began setting Aunt Gladys's editorial while Angie began to lay the story into the chase that already contained the flag and masthead. Swiftly she replaced the date and volume number, thus announcing a new edition.

By nine, she was proofing the editorial, and he was simultaneously setting corrections by looking over her shoulder. By nine-thirty they were proofing the entire front page and making some final alterations.

She sighed. "Well, Mr. Purser, this went slower than I'd hoped, but here we are. I'll show you some of the peculiarities of this press."

He nodded. She had started to relax a little. Marty, bless the young man, had seen to her needs after all.

She ran a hand truck carrying page four to the press and gently slid the rear page from the steel surface of the truck onto the flat plane of the press, pushing it into place.

"All right, Mr. Purser, page one now."

He pushed vigorously, straight toward a

crowbar lying in its path. The truck smacked into the crowbar, careened wildly, and slowly righted itself. But not before the heavy chase, containing the entire front page, slid lazily, ominously, toward the right side and then avalanched over the side, landing with a roar that shivered the entire building. It flopped on a corner, spun, and dropped with a clang.

Type flew everywhere, followed by pounds of leading and big display letters. The flag, cast from typemetal, skidded across the ink-black floor to rest at the foot of the press.

Angie watched, horrified, unable to stop the unfolding disaster. Purser stared, aghast, shaking his head. "Oh, oh, oh," he bawled.

It was nearly ten o'clock. The newsboys would deliver the paper at seven the next morning, in time for breakfast.

She eyed the crowbar, lying fatefully on the floor near the press, and knew she had not put it there.

"Mr. Purser, come with me to the front desk," she said.

He followed. She opened the cash drawer, calculated swiftly, and handed him three dollars. "That more than covers your typesetting at sixty cents for a thousand ems. I will no longer require your services. You may go."

"No, no, I wouldn't think of it. Your son pays me. I report to him, ma'am. I'll help you put things proper," he said.

"You will go, Mr. Purser."

But he ignored her. Instead, he returned to the press area and began brooming type into a pile. She let him.

First they would sort every piece of type and return it to its nest in the case boxes. Then she would set the front page herself, probably in abbreviated form, using some filler. With luck she could print in the morning and the paper would be delivered before evening.

As soon as they had restored the type to the case boxes, she intended to escort the compositor to the door and force the issue if she had to.

So this was Marty's gift to his mother.

CHAPTER 16

Marty, oh, Marty . . .

Angie scooped handfuls of pied type and non-pareil slugs from the ink-blacked planks and dropped them on the compositor's bench while Mr. Purser flipped the font into the upper and lower case boxes in the sullen light of the smoking kerosene lamp overhead.

Ink ran in Marty's blood, and he knew how fragile and sacred was the voice of a newspaper. Marty's first trundle bed stood beside a press, and his first lullaby had been the clank of the platen. Marty, her own Marty, had dirtied his diapers with printer's ink, accompanied his mother on her rounds, learned the English tongue so well he was now an eloquent and forceful politician.

Marty, betraying all he respected, everything she had taught him about honor, virtue, the sacred mission to defend the commonwealth against dark lights, the sacrament of each and every newspaper in a perfidious world. She would not let this stranger see her tears and choked them back.

She grieved as she scraped up the pied type and dragged the heavy chase off the floor and onto a stone so she could rebuild the front page. The lamp would burn its coal oil all night.

She eyed the compositor, certain the disaster had been ordained by her own son even though it had appeared to be an accident.

"Mr. Purser, when you're done with the sorting, you may leave. I plan to set type all night, and I'll do the rest."

"I couldn't do that, ma'am. I'll stay."

"I will do the typesetting, and I will load the press."

He smiled and nodded.

When at last he had flipped the last letter into the last compartment, she pulled her story off the spike, grabbed the type stick, and began setting it once again while he hovered in the darkness. She had often worked in semi-dark, setting stories through the long hours of night. The skill hadn't come easily. A compositor set a story one letter at a time, the letters sliding onto the stick right to left and upside down. She scarcely needed to see, not until it was time to proof the typeset lines.

But now, as her hands mechanically plucked letters from their cubicles, she sensed something was wrong, and a deepening dread infused her. She set a dozen lines while the man hovered about, and then stopped. She lifted the galley tray up to the buttery light and read what she had written.

Very little of it made sense.

She sighed, defeated. Marty's man had flipped

the letters into the wrong nests, upper and lower cases mixed as well as all the letters and numbers in the entire font. It was late. She had a nonpareil font if she cared to set in six-point type, and she had a part of a font of larger letters. If she tried the other fonts, he would find ways to thwart her.

She felt as weary as she ever had been.

"You win tonight," she said. "Plug it and print."

"It's a blasphemy," he said, enigmatically.

He pulled precast filler material off the shelves, stories cast in typemetal and bonded to wood to bring them to the proper height. She had mounds of that stuff, mostly stories with barely concealed advertising in them, handed out gratis by various commerce-minded concerns. There was a preset three-column by eight-inch story about circuses, mentioning P. T. Barnum's prominently several times. A canned story about women's assorted ailments featured Lydia Pinkham's Vegetable Compound. In fact, most of the filler material had been supplied by patent medicine companies.

Swiftly, Purser set to work, whistling "Yankee Doodle" and patriotic riffs as he dropped blocks of material onto the front page and added "furniture," wood blocks that would show as white space on the paper, to fit all together. Barnum, Lydia Pinkham, Dr. Sage's Catarrh Remedy, Sutherland Sisters' Hair Grower, Dr. Kilmer's

Cough Remedy, all artfully woven into stories.

"Blasphemy," he muttered. "Saints presarve us."

Building the page took him only minutes, and then he rolled the truck to the press and slid that appalling front page onto the flatbed. She watched miserably as he whipped through a printing, his big muscles conquering the task in a quarter of the time she usually spent running an edition.

He chortled and clucked as he worked, mirth rising from somewhere within his inky soul. His seamed face betrayed comedy, triumph, supercilious joy, craftiness, victory. It wasn't even late when he plucked the last sheet; eleven-thirty. Time enough for Marty's bought man to soak up his hundred-proof reward at the Lone Star Saloon, basking in Marty's praise.

She watched him wipe down the press, doff his ragtag apron, and scrub his perfidious hands. In the morning she would call the constable and have this intruder, who was ravaging her paper, ejected. But the very thought triggered a foreknowledge of what Spade Ball would or wouldn't do.

Nonetheless, she would try. She might seek a restraining order from Sid Wannamaker's court, prohibiting the man from entering her business establishment — but she knew what the justice would and wouldn't do. Marty's ring ran Opportunity, but she would try, and let their shame fall upon them.

Bleakly she waited for the intruder to finish his toilet. Then she turned down the wick until the lamp blued out and followed the man to the door.

"See you upon the morrow, madam," he said cheerfully.

She didn't reply. With her skeleton key she locked her door and plunged into the oppressive night.

So Marty had won. She no longer controlled her own paper. He had known exactly what to do and did it. She felt desolated by it all. Her own son, an able newsman and printer in his own right, the scion of two upright news people who had devoted their lives not only to making a living with their press, but to bettering the communities in which they published. Now her boy's very name rolled bitterly across her mind.

As she trudged home in the suffocating dark, the sound of a rinky-dink piano drifted to her from the cowboy quarter. The boys from Texas managed to enjoy themselves even when beset by the birds of carrion who roosted in Opportunity, her son among them.

She felt the weight of failure crushing her. Not the failure to publish the stories she had written, but that deeper failure, to arm Marty with the moral and spiritual strengths he would need to lead a good and blameless life.

A mother's failure. She had dodged that reality for years, pretended Marty wasn't what he was. She had tried to slough it off on his choice of bad company; blame anything, everything but herself. But now she could no longer escape it: she had failed her son.

The boy had grown up in a newsroom, along with his dead sister. Had she been too busy to give him what any little boy needed? Guiltily she remembered the swift hugs, the cross rebuffs when she was busy, the long absences when she was out hawking ads or gathering news, leaving the child to fend for himself with only his busy father on hand.

Had she schooled him? Marty had never needed a school. By osmosis he had absorbed a fine education in those newspapers; he had a broad vocabulary, perfect spelling, a fine way of composing a story or letter, an advanced knowledge of mathematics, a good command of civics, an understanding of history and politics, and a keen grasp of the foibles of the world, for all things flowed through his childish life each day.

But she had failed, and now that failure burdened her so much that she could scarcely breathe. She had not kept an eye on her son when he was old enough to roam. She had never introduced him to the faith she had grown up with. They had never found or attended a church. It had been enough that she and her husband should keep watch over the secular world, so Marty had never heard a sermon nor had he ever examined the Bible or understood how its sacred texts governed everything in the world.

She had failed him. That's all she knew that night, and the thought rebuked her soul and caused a shortness of breath in her weary body.

She wasn't particularly tired. Usually, the business of strong-arming that press exhausted her. But the whiskey printer had done that, set the stories, shoved the heavy trucks around. It wasn't even midnight.

At home at last, she poured some sun tea she had percolated all that summer day and sipped the tepid brew, drawing strength from it. She settled in her rocker and tried to think things through.

She might try to publish in Topeka and bring the papers in on the railroad. But Marty knew about those old dodges, and so would that bought-and-paid-for printer, and they would be eyeing her every move, ready to intercept copy going out and printed editions coming in on the railroad express cars. The chances of doing editions out of town were negligible, but really her only choice.

The only other option was to set type when the printer was sleeping, working in the wee hours and hiding the galleys of type somewhere until she could print a small edition alone, also in the wee hours, when only the marshal or his deputies roamed the silent streets.

She laughed helplessly. The depleted type in the caseboxes would alert that printer. The night-owl lamp would alert the constables, and Marty would know of her efforts.

She took heart. There had to be a way.

Her thoughts focused on her friend the postmaster. Horatio Bates was an odd duck, owl-eyed and shrewd, slovenly yet wise. It occurred to her that with his help and the assistance of the United States mails, she might still produce editions of *The Outlook* that Marty wouldn't know about until too late.

If she succeeded, would it do any good? Was Opportunity too parasitic to reform itself? Were its merchants too venal? Was Marty's machine too corrupt? She could think of fifty good people in town, people who could make a difference if inspired by truth and indignation. She would try to reach them.

She drained the last of the tea and slipped into bed, no longer feeling the oppression that deviled her. She knew she hadn't failed Marty. She and Gideon had instilled moral and ethical courage in the boy, rebuked his childhood fibs, encouraged industry and honesty.

Marty had failed himself. Maybe she hadn't been the best of mothers, rearing the lad in a print shop, but she had taught him the nature of good and evil, loved him dearly, took pride in his successes, and brought him to manhood. No, he had betrayed himself with bad moral choices.

Now she hoped to redeem him. That would be the ultimate maternal love.

CHAPTER 17

Angie found Marshal Ball propped behind his desk, cleaning his Peacemaker.

"Been expecting you," he said, sighting down the shining barrel at her.

"I've got a trespasser," she said. "I want that tramp printer removed from my shop."

He grinned. "The mayor, he says it's a family squabble. I ain't supposed to get into it."

She fumed. "I am the sole owner and proprietor of *The Outlook*. Marty doesn't own one sliver of it. Now you come with me and boot that soak-brained compositor out of my place and keep him out."

"That'd be disturbing the peace, ma'am."

"Get off your duff and do your sworn duty, Spade, or the whole damned world's going to hear about it."

He smirked. "Tell you what. You go fetch me a say-so from hizzoner, and I'll take you up on it. I like to pick on vagrants. It's like cleaning rats out of town."

He ran an oily piece of a longjohn's trapdoor through the chambers in the cylinder and then reloaded the fat, short rounds with a cheery clinking.

She stared at him, defeated. Where else could she turn if not the law? But she was not done with him. "I've been gagged. You and Marty think you have me where you want me. You figure you can go on looting those cowboys, taking away their cash. Some for the city, some for your pockets.

"But it's all going to catch up with you someday. Maybe soon, maybe a long time from now when you look back on your life, and you feel ashamed of it.

"You could have stood up and been counted for something, but you chose another path, and all I know is, you'll regret that path. We all regret a wrong path, Spade."

He laughed, clicked the cylinder back into the frame of the revolver, and whirled it. The gesture had its effect.

She knew that what she said to him would devil him. He would wake up in the deeps of some night and remember her little homily and wonder whether he was doing the right thing with his life. The world was full of Spade Balls, whose triumphs were purely temporary, and whose destruction lasted a lifetime.

She stormed over to city hall, where Sid Wannamaker held court, dispensing injustice the way some men dispensed bad whiskey, and fattening his purse along with the city's.

He wasn't in. His duties rarely usurped a half hour of his day. But she knew where to find him, and headed for Wanda's Café next door, where he coffeed with his cronies all day long in a mustard-tinted rear room.

She worked her way to the rear table where he was reading yesterday's *Kansas City Star*, along with his pals.

"Well, if it isn't the pert little lady from the paper," he said. "I guess you're after a story. Nope, I didn't hang nobody today, but I've a mind to."

His cronies chortled.

"I would like a court order," she said without preamble. "I want you to restrain someone who's trespassing in my shop."

"Oh, him. He's there to keep little grannies from being rambunctious," he said. "He's a wholesome influence on you. Women take some steadying, don't you think?"

"Will you write a restraining order or not?"

Wannamaker shrugged. "It's a family difficulty. The man's wage is being paid by your son."

"No, it's not a family matter. I own the paper. All of it."

His eyes danced. "Well, I think not. That printer's keeping your paper sober and upright and temperate and wise and lawful. I'd hate to see you libel someone. Now, if he was busy hellfiring and damnationing everyone in government, I might take offense at the man. But he's just the remedy for an excess of temperament of the female variety. I think he's good medicine, anti-inflammatory and cathartic, like castor oil."

This was running the way she had expected.

"Very well, Sid. But your conscience is going to haunt you. You could listen to your ideals. You could still be counted as one of the fine pioneers who settled this place. You could be remembered for your courage and fairness and sense of justice for all, no matter how humble. You have a chance to shine, Sid."

He chuckled. "You sure are fancy with words," he said.

She left the café, having made her point. He could laugh all he wanted, but her talk about conscience and justice and fairness would rest heavily within him.

But that didn't give her back her paper.

She headed next for the Lone Star Saloon, walking through a peaceful morning. In this cowboy side of town, delivery wagons owned the street each morning. The hour hand had not yet attacked nine, but she intended to wake up Marty.

But strangely, he was already up, dressed, and in the saloon.

"I've been expecting you," he said from his ornate office just off the bar.

"I want that man out, right now."

"There's nothing you can do about it, so stop trying."

"I will never stop trying, Marty."

He beamed. "Then you'll just wear yourself out."

"Marty, there's something that separates us. I

have a conscience and you don't. I am pursuing justice and fairness, and —"

"Don't come around here and preach, or I'll have you thrown out."

"I am going to preach, because that's what was lacking in your life. I wish now that I had taken you to hear some preaching because it would have saved you this . . . this shame. You're corrupt and unjust. You're bringing shame upon your good name, and upon our family name. I wish . . ."

He sighed, stood, circumnavigated his desk, shuffled to the door, and gestured.

A moment later a burly barkeep with a waxed mustache and center-parted black hair propelled her toward the swinging doors as easily as if she had been a down-filled pillow. Not even when she refused to put one foot ahead of the other did he slow. He simply lifted her out to the manure-shot street and left her in the dazzling sunlight.

"Stay away," Marty said from the doorway.

"I wasn't a good mother," she said, "but now I intend to be."

She worked her way around a beer wagon, a meat wagon, and other conveyances, and left Lone Star Street behind her.

Back in her office she felt oppressed. The printer was cheerfully sorting the type he had pied the previous night. She eyed him dourly. Did no one in Opportunity possess an ordinary conscience?

She discovered that Gladys Busby had prepared the advertising invoices, addressed the exchange papers, sold three cards and two small display ads, and taken two stories and an obituary, but not even that good news lifted her spirits.

She collected the exchanges and headed for the post office, glad to escape the sullied altar of her workplace, profaned by that unwelcome galoot in the back room. The edition shamed her. She examined it as she hiked to the post office, despising the mixed typefaces, the efflorescent patent medicine ads barely disguised as news stories, and the whole gallimaufry.

She laid the bundle on Mr. Bates's counter and glared at him, daring him to say one word. But he did.

"It's a very strange edition," he said, thumbing the papers.

"Pied type," she said shortly. "Filler."

"You've abandoned your little crusade to reform this town?"

"None of your business."

"Oh, oh my." He refused to look at her, his gaze darting floorward and ceilingward. He totted up the postage, she paid, and she started to huff out the door when he stayed her.

"Angie? No one around. Could you spare a moment?"

She desperately wanted to visit with him, but fought it. She didn't want the world to know what had happened to *The Outlook*. Against her better judgment, she allowed herself to push through the little swinging gate and settle across from him in his inner sanctum behind the wicket.

"Some things are worth fighting for," he said.

"Who says I've quit?" she shot back.

"I should mind my own business."

"Yes, you damn well should."

"Is Mrs. Busby working out?"

"Splendidly."

"I thought she would. That's why I recommended her. Did she pie the type?"

"None of your business, Horatio."

"You are not your usual self."

"Thanks for the compliment." She arose, determined to flee the nosy old man, but halted at the door.

"I'm a prisoner," she said.

He nodded her back to her seat. She sat down stonily, wondering why she was about to feed the town's gossip mill, and then told Bates the whole story.

He sighed. "I knew it was something like that. Maybe I can help."

"How?"

"Things come and go in the U.S. Mail. Stories can be written at home and mailed to Topeka or someplace where they print; galley proofs can come by mail from distant places and be proofed in your own home. Whole issues can come by parcel service or railway express, ready for your newsboys to pick up at your house. All that's required of a postmaster is utter silence. That is the one gift I can offer. Secrecy."

"Thanks, Horatio, but Marty's aware of every trick. And so is that tramp printer. They know all about publishing an issue out of town, and they'll be waiting for me to move."

He grinned. "I like conspiracies."

She smiled back. "I'm game," she said. "But don't count on anything yet. I'm not ready to print out of town, not now."

"Tampering with the mail's a federal offense, Angie. You put a postage stamp on some mail and suddenly things are different. Marty knows it, and so do the cops."

"It might work — once. One issue."

"Once may be all you need. Angie, I plum admire you. I just knew you wouldn't cave in. You've got something inside of you, this sense of justice, of fairness, of what's right. You care so much about these things that not even your son —"

"Horatio, don't you say it! Marty's my flesh and blood. I raised him, I love him, and I'll try to help him past his mistakes. I want his administration to succeed, not fail."

He gazed solemnly at her. "That's what makes you such a marvel, Angie Drum," he said, gently. "One in a million."

She didn't know why the hell she was crying.

CHAPTER 18

It was time for a powwow. Addison McCoy had always dodged politics. He brokered livestock and his business ran smooth as pearls when he steered clear of partisan passions. But this hot and brooding summer Mayor Drum's machine found him and clamped its jaws on him and shook him like a mastiff shakes a rabbit.

All that summer he had placated angry herd bosses and cowboys who threatened to blow the town to bits if Drum's kangaroo court didn't lay off, and Drum's city marshal didn't stop pocketing every penny a drover had on him. Twice he had gone to Marty Drum and told him that someday soon the town would face the consequences.

Homeward-bound cowboys who had been unjustly bilked had been talking to northbound cowboys and trail bosses, and the most recent hands to arrive on the bedding grounds south of town were primed for trouble and looking for it. They'd learned to keep their cash in camp instead of pocketing three or four months of trail wages. A big evening in Opportunity meant putting four bits in their jeans. And that had suddenly lessened the receipts that Sid Wannamaker

146

was extracting from them and lowered the take for Spade Ball even more.

The result was that Ball and his minions were nabbing cowboys even more ruthlessly and with less excuse than ever, which only fueled the rage down on Lone Star Street and in the cow camps out of town.

Worse, Ball had taken to nabbing the trail bosses themselves on some miserable excuse or another because they were usually carrying cash, often wages they intended to distribute to their men. What had started as a method of milking the visitors had turned into a racket, and word about Opportunity blazed from one camp to another south of town.

The last six trail bosses that McCoy had dealt with ended up before Judge Wannamaker on some scabrous charge or other, and if they happened to be carrying payroll for their men, Ball pocketed an extra ten or fifteen dollars as "jail costs." McCoy heard plenty. There would be no trail herds coming to Opportunity next year unless this abuse stopped. The Texans would drive to Abilene and the Kansas Pacific even if it was three or four days farther.

And the last two trail bosses, Bill Timmons and Barney Noble, had raged at the town, at Drum, at the thieving lawmen, and sworn that Hash Brown would even the score. McCoy had listened carefully, thinking about his working capital in the bank, thinking about the hundreds of Texans bilked and humiliated by Ball's iron law enforcement. Only Spade's reputation as a master shootist spared him deadly confrontations.

Hash Brown's two outfits were crawling north somewhere, two weeks to a month out, and primed for revenge. That's what every Texan on the Chisholm Trail was waiting for. Hash Brown's men were Confederate veterans, experienced pistoleers, ruthless, lawless, unprincipled, and more than willing to level Opportunity right to the bare earth with gunpowder, fire, and sword.

That's what separated Brown's riders from the usual cheerful boys learning the cattle business; boys who used their ancient sixguns to pound horseshoe nails and kill snakes and maybe signal one another for help.

McCoy wanted to talk to Marty Drum alone, away from those cronies he was always giving the crumbs off his table. But when McCoy pierced the Lone Star Saloon, he realized this was going to be a public discussion. Drum hunkered at his usual rear table flanked by Spade Ball and Arnie Marlowe. A few Texas cowboys decorated the bar, just to add cordite to the conference.

Ball was there. Maybe that was good.

"Howya?" asked Drum, motioning McCoy to an empty chair. The broker took it.

"We'll talk, public or private, you choose."

Drum grinned and winked at his coterie.

"There's trouble coming up that trail, Marty."

"So I've heard."

"More trouble than you know. I'm not talking about Hash Brown. Not yet, anyway. I'm talking about the herds. They may be quitting us. I hear that one's turned toward Kansas City. They're going to cut east and keep on going another hundred fifty miles just to spite this town. They've had it. Word's gone down that trail faster than word came up it, and word is, no one's getting a fair shake in Opportunity."

"That's not likely, McCoy."

"It's happening right now. Three or four more herds coming in, then Hash Brown's two — he's somewhere down there, coming closer each day — and that's the end of the cattle business in Opportunity. Maybe it's the end of Opportunity."

Ball chuckled. Drum smiled pensively.

"They'll come back next year," the mayor said. "They're not that dumb, going three weeks more, wearing pounds off their beef."

"No, Marty, it's cheaper to lose some herd weight than it is to lose their cash here. That's pure economics."

Spade Ball was enjoying himself. "Looks like we'll have to ride out onto the prairie and usher 'em in."

"Your jurisdiction ends at the city limits, Ball."

"You sound like you ain't happy. You want to say so to my face? I'm listening."

McCoy let it pass. The man was baiting him. He turned to the mayor. "There's still time.

There's two outfits in town right now. Treat 'em right. If Ball runs them through court for no good reason, get Wannamaker to reverse his rulings and return the cash." He stared at Ball. "And you could return every penny you've cleaned out of their pockets."

The Texas boys at the bar were sure listening hard. McCoy liked that.

"You could send refunds down the trail, Ball. I bet those boys there would make sure it goes to the right men and the right outfits. Only you know whose pockets you've picked, so —"

"I don't like that kind of talk."

"Well I'm talking it. You can return your plunder, or you can sit back and see how Hash Brown's going to take it from you."

Ball smiled gently. "He's in for some surprises."

Drum sat there, his eyes hooded, calculating. "Are you with us, McCoy?"

"What do you mean?"

"You for my administration or not? You haven't paid us any dues, but you've sure cleaned up the business. Gotten rich off of Opportunity."

McCoy decided to make his views plain. "I'm for doing what's right and honorable. If you do what's right, I'm with you. If you just keep on bilking the Texans, I'll move west. Railroad's going to ship from Dodge City pretty smartly now. This town's about to fade away even if Hash Brown doesn't kick it to perdition."

Marty Drum stared at the wagonwheel chandelier. "You know, McCoy, we're thinking of raising the fees the city charges for those loading pens. Ten cents isn't enough for that. Me and Arnie here, we're thinking it should be fifty cents next year."

"There won't be a next year, Marty, unless things change."

"Who needs cattle? We'll be a county seat. We'll beat out Hutchinson; that's what they're saying in Topeka."

McCoy stood. There was little more to say. Marty Drum, emboldened by his cronies and drink, hadn't absorbed the warning.

He walked coldly across the hollow room and into clean sunlight. The limestone Merchant Bank of Opportunity, on the corner of Kansas Street and Second, would be his next stop.

He discovered the man he wanted to see, Magnus Garrity, barricaded behind his six-foot-wide desk. Garrity favored distance in social and business situations, and the beeswaxed desk supplied it. McCoy sat himself down uninvited while Garrity huffed an insincere welcome and glared into his papers a long moment.

"Magnus, I'll get right to the needle. If you want a functioning bank in a functioning town next year, you're going to have to act fast."

Garrity's arctic gaze settled on the broker through frost-lidded eyes, but he said nothing.

"I'm talking about Marty Drum's Ring, and I'm talking about the Texas herds. This is it,

Magnus. This town reforms, right now, this week, before this shipping season ends, or else you won't see many herds arriving next year. You won't see me, either. I'll be moving to Dodge City, where the western herds are coming."

"Melodramatic, Addison."

"No, Magnus. Several of the trail bosses told me so. They're not coming back. Their boys get bilked by the constables and justice court. Sometimes Ball and Wannamaker clean out an outfit's entire payroll, cash money the herd bosses paid to these Texans, and the boys head south penniless after all the risk and danger and work and expense of bringing cattle here, without even a good time to show for it."

McCoy spotted no thaw at all in that glacial face.

"We pay no taxes," the banker said, and settled back into his self-comfort.

McCoy knew that Garrity was one of Mayor Drum's key supporters — and maybe one of the beneficiaries of Drum's Ring.

"Magnus, look at it from the business angle. We may be the closest railroad town from Texas, but we're the most expensive to ship from, thanks to Spade Ball and the rest. It makes no sense for those Texans to ship from here. That's simple business sense."

The banker turned schoolmasterish. "This fall the legislature will make us the county seat. There'll be courthouse business. Not one merchant in town is counting on cattle shipping to last more than another two or three years. Not the way the railroads are building. We'll be at the center of a wheat farming and hog raising empire."

Garrity turned to his papers, dismissing the broker with a gesture. But McCoy refused to be dismissed.

"Magnus, I'm going to tell you what's about to happen this year, not next. Hash Brown's coming here in a few weeks with two big herds and about thirty tough men. Every broke Texas cowboy heading south's been feeding Brown stories about bad treatment in Opportunity.

"When Brown gets here, anything could happen. One of those anythings is the armed robbery of this bank. I'd say that's at the top of the list. Every Texas cowboy heading south knows that this big black safe, right here, is where his hard-won trail wage ended up, posted to various accounts, especially Drum's and Ball's."

Garrity coughed.

"Smart people are going to pull their cash from here before Brown arrives. Some smart people might even close their businesses before then. What I'm saying, Magnus, is that there's time to turn this around . . . if you have the courage and vision to do so."

CHAPTER 19

With Aunt Gladys manning the front office and Mr. Purser slinging type, Angie at last found time to pursue the corruption story. She didn't yet know how she would present that story to the public, but she would find a way. For now, she was content to dig.

Sid Wannamaker and Spade Ball wouldn't even let her into their lairs, much less examine public records. So she had to work from the other end, interviewing the victims. At first she posted herself at the bridge over the Arkansas River, hoping to talk to cowboys drifting in and out of the camps south of town. But then Eddie Farrar chased her off, tore up her notes, and told her he would pinch her if she loitered there.

She chose instead to rent a horse and trap from Billy de Vere, who sourly harnessed a gentle mare and charged her twice what he normally did. She minded, but didn't protest because she needed that rig.

She drove the trap over the thundering plank bridge and into a fine August day, still hot, but dry now, with playful zephyrs toying with browned grasses. She had never been in a Texas cow camp, and scarcely knew what to expect.

She did know that vast herds of longhorns were bedded along the south bank of the river, sometimes ten or fifteen miles from town, and that the drovers continued to care for the longhorns until they could be shipped by the overburdened Santa Fe Railroad.

And she surmised that around each of those cookfires, she would discover seething rage, bitterness — and stories. She wanted those stories, but wasn't sure how to get them. She was, after all, the mayor's mother.

She turned west and drove across open prairie toward a distant herd that milled restlessly on a long slope, held by circling drovers. The sun penetrated her thin cotton dress, and she was grateful for the wide-rimmed straw hat that protected her fair skin from burn. She knew she looked pretty in it, which she hoped would help her get her story. She doubted that any of those cowboys had ever seen a woman in camp.

She located the chuckwagon on the lee side of a gentle slope, as far out of the west wind as possible. She saw picketed horses standing three-legged in the breeze, and various men lazing in the sun. It struck her as a delightful life, at least when the weather suited them.

She rode slowly, not wanting to stir up the restless herd, and passed hundreds of strange-looking cattle; black, brown, brindle, cream, gray, red, mottled, spotted, and all with fantastic horns of all shapes.

Then at last she reached the camp and

stopped. Men scrambled to their feet. Some were shirtless. The cook stopped scrubbing a black pot. All looked lean and hard-used. They gawked, as she knew they would. She weathered their stares with dignity.

"I'm looking for the man in charge," she said.

No one responded for a moment, so she addressed the nearest man, a lean, sunbaked kid chinned with a scraggle of beard. "Are you the boss?"

"Reckon not, ma'am. He's in town."

"What outfit is this?"

"The Pitchfork, ma'am, out of San Marcos."

"And the owner?"

"Joe Bass. He's doing some banking, I reckon."

"Do you suppose I could have a little visit with some of you?"

"Well, we ain't proper here. I mean . . ."

"That doesn't matter a bit. I want to talk about something that is troubling us all."

The cowboy looked dubious.

"There's things happening in town that I don't like."

That evoked laughter in some, dark glares in others. But no one responded.

"I'm talking about law enforcement."

The blond kid squinted. "I think you'd better git on, ma'am."

"Please hear me out."

They didn't reply, but shuffled close enough to hear. So she told them who she was, what she was trying to do, and that she wanted their stories. Any abuse or injustice or unfairness. Dates, times, amounts, sentences, bail — everything.

"You say your name's Drum, is it? Like the mayor?"

"He's my son, and we don't see eye to eye on this."

"Blood's thicker'n water, ma'am."

"Marty's wrong. His City Hall Ring is wrong. His constables are cheating you. Do you want to help me, or not? I'm the only person in Opportunity who can do something about it."

Deep silence. The air between her and these boys was thick. Then the blond kid replied for them all. "I guess we ain't saying anything to you, ma'am. Not unless Joe Bass says so."

"I want to help. I want to publish every injustice I come across. I can't see police records or court records, even though they're supposed to be public. I don't have access to the town's ledgers, even though those are public, too. My own son does his best to silence me. Unless you tell me about justice in my town, I can't help you."

"I guess you'd just better turn that rig around and leave us alone, lady," the youth said.

She surrendered. "What's the next camp?"

"Bar L, yonder. Out of Waco."

"How far?"

"Don't rightly know."

She left, feeling the rolling wall of bitterness hustle her away. She put the brown mare into a jog and steered again over open prairie, seeing no sign of a cow camp or herd to the west. She veered southwest after a while, and happened suddenly upon the camp lying in a broad grassy valley. She had come a far piece from Opportunity.

They were just as startled to discover a female among them here as before, and she knew better how to handle it. Let 'em look, or dive for their shirts, or perform their hasty toilet.

This herd looked much like the other, with big rangy longhorns scattered across the valley, most of them quiet and better fed and watered than the other herd. She headed for the cookfire again, noting that this outfit didn't have a chuckwagon, preferring a pair of smaller utility wagons.

This time a gray-bearded veteran of the outdoors greeted her cordially.

"Rafe Lamb," he said. "This here's the entire wealth, future, and prospects of yours truly. These here are my boys, all of us from Waco, if you know where that is. You up to some coffee thick enough to float a muleshoe?"

"I think I am. Are you up to doing something daring?"

"Never was a dare that Rafe Lamb didn't consider," he said, his eyes all question.

She alighted and dropped the carriage weight next to the mare.

"All right, I'm going to do some fast talking, and when I come up for air, you can tell me if it's yes or no."

She did talk, eloquently, driven by her hopes

for Opportunity, driven by her loathing of the corruption and venalty she was witnessing there, driven by her knife-edged love of justice and hatred of injustice. She talked about her son, and the sundering of their lives, and her grief, and how he was thwarting her, and how she feared for him and the whole town. And then she talked about the story she had in mind: names, dates, amounts, experiences, everything that would make a case and inspire reforms.

"So there it is. You willing?"

Lamb burrowed into his shirt pocket for a black cheroot, scraped a lucifer across his britches, and lit up.

"Luke, you come over heah and tell the lady your troubles."

The drover named Luke, a short man with handlebars as wide as his head, stepped forward. He swallowed air, puffed up, and then released the cargo in his lungs.

"Well, ma'am, I was counting on some good times on Lone Star Street, getting that trail dust outta my parched throat, and Mr. Lamb, he comes into camp after dickering the cattle away, and he lets the half of us go on in. He's heard about Spade Ball and the justice court, so he warns us to behave, and not take more'n ten dollars or we'd for sure lose our trail wage.

"Well, I took ten and hid another ten in my boot, where that marshal, he don't see it. And we ride in one evening and order up a round of

159

redeye at the Lone Star Saloon, all peaceful-like, keeping an eye out for this marshal.

"It ain't much of a story, ma'am. I drink down two to take the parch out of me and think maybe I'll try the Palace two doors down, and I get Jimmy Gans here to go with me. No sooner does we put foot on the street than Spade Ball comes down on us and says we're disturbing the peace, drunk and disorderly, and resisting arrest. He says we'd better come quietly or he'll charge us with vagrant, too.

"So, feeling a little peeved, I said we was no more disturbing the peace than that yellow dog lying there on the boardwalk. And Ball, he rants and raves and threatens worse, and we end up in that stinking jail of his, where we were stuck all night with nothing but a bucket of water and a slop pail.

"Next morning, he comes in and makes us pull out our pockets, and he sees seven dollars and change in mine. That's for the court, he says. Then he says we should pull off our boots, and, quick as a snake, he's got the ten I hid in there, and he's making jokes about how bad the ten dollars smell. Then he hauls us all down the street to the city hall, and we go before the JP, Wannamaker, and he says we can go if we make bail for twenty-five dollars. None of us has that, so he takes whatever we've got, lets us loose, and that's how I was cleaned out. I don't reckon I did one wrong thing."

Angie scribbled that down.

"Next, you, Willis," yelled Lamb.

Angie knew she would hear a lot of stories that morning.

CHAPTER 20

In the space of an hour, Angie recorded the whole sorry treatment of the boys in that camp. One by one, at Rafe Lamb's behest, they spilled their stories. In all, eight of the fourteen men in that outfit had been nabbed by Spade Ball and fined by Sid Wannamaker.

All eight had been pinched on the cowboy side of town, usually on Lone Star Street, and most often at night. Those who had escaped included the cook, Wiggins, who had driven in broad daylight to the mercantile on Kansas Street and bought provisions for the homeward journey. Others, riding straight past the rough district, had been able to purchase items for their own kits, get a haircut at a tonsorial parlor, send mail, or do some banking without trouble.

Two of those were nondrinkers, studious youths with a demeanor about them that contrasted sharply with the easy camaraderie of the others.

Of those caught by the city marshal or his deputies, only one, Randy Morgan, confessed to owning a little too much redeye when he was pinched. But he insisted he had been doing nothing wrong and was only walking toward his horse to ride back to camp. They had charged him with vagrancy, of all things.

When she asked what had happened after they were thrown into the stinking cell, she got different answers. Apparently Ball had no particular mode of dealing with the Texans. But one thing became clear: he usually made sure the court, and the city, got in ahead of him, and he picked up the leavings. That made sense. Ball was being careful to feed his superiors first and pocket what was left over.

Another thing became plain. Some of the cowboys were flat broke when they were pinched. The judge always threatened them with ten days in jail, which commonly resulted in having others ante up either the forfeited bail or the fine, and that usually meant fetching Lamb, who had to ride in to spring his men. There had not been a single trial.

Angie made careful notes, describing the events in acute and damning detail, leaving nothing out — if she could find some way to get this story into print.

"Thank you," she said. "Now I have one last question for you all: you and the other Texans, hundreds of you, have been maltreated. Why haven't you fought back? Why are you taking all this lying down? You gents love a good brawl. What's happening?"

She discovered only dead silence and only observed the masks that slid swiftly over the faces of these young hellions.

Finally Rafe Lamb replied. "I suppose, ma'am, it's up to the trail boss and the owner of this outfit to answer that. There are several reasons.

"One is that Ball is one of the finest shootists in the world and deserves the respect he gets. He's a one-man army. Another is that town ordinances prevent us from wearing sidearms in town."

She listened skeptically. At times there had been two or three hundred Texans on Lone Star Street — against only the city marshal and his two deputies.

"I don't buy it," she said.

Lamb grinned. "The Avenger is coming. The boys are waiting for Hash Brown to correct these wrongs."

"How?"

Lamb just smiled and shook his head.

"Ma'am," volunteered one of the youths, "when Brown's done, there won't be one building standing in Opportunity. There ain't even going to be any track running through it."

That chilled her. "I see. Do all the outfits believe this?"

"Believe it! They're all counting on it!"

She was listening to a death warrant.

She wished she might tarry, visit other outfits, but she had what she needed and the paper still required her presence.

"I will do my best to right the wrongs, repay what has been taken, and make Opportunity a place where you all will be glad to come and have a good time," she said.

No one said much. They plainly didn't believe she could do it.

She rode slowly back to Opportunity, taking care to conceal her notes in her chemise before entering town. She knew the marshal or his deputies would be scrutinizing her, looking for anything they might find. Only the fact that she was Marty Drum's mother kept them from playing a rougher game.

She returned the trap to Billy de Vere, who squinted suspiciously at her, studied the dray mare for abuse, and silently led the horse to her stall.

She had a story. She still had the previous week's story, and Mrs. Busby's acid editorial. The trick now was to publish what she knew and trust that the sober and honorable citizens of Opportunity would react — and do so in time. The whole town and every citizen in it were in jeopardy. She had always trusted an informed public to act. But this time, with taxes at stake, she wondered.

She walked stiffly toward the paper under the lingering gaze of deputy Farrar, aware that the paper stuffed in her bosom raised odd bulges in the wrong places.

Everything seemed normal enough at *The Outlook*. In the rear, Fox Purser was cheerfully setting type, a wad of tobacco lodged in his cheek. At the front, the formidable Aunt Gladys

Busby was churning out church news of a christening, a report of a wagon wreck, a story about the falling price of cattle because of gluts in the stockyards, and similar items.

Tonight they would put the paper to bed, with or without her corruption stories. That meant dealing with Fox Purser, one way or another. She laid her notes on her desk and chatted with Gladys while trying to decide how to approach him.

But she already knew. She must first take the high road. That meant appealing to his conscience and treating him as a responsible man.

She headed back to the shop and addressed him: "Mr. Purser, please come to my desk," she said in a tone of voice that brooked no argument.

The itinerant printer set down his type stick and followed her. He had that cockiness she had often seen in big males who seemed to enjoy towering over smaller women.

"Please sit," she said sharply, motioning him to the sole chair on the public side of her cluttered desk.

"Mr. Purser, I wish to appeal to your conscience," she said.

A certain wariness lit his red-veined face, though his gaze remained bland.

"This paper is struggling to reform a city that is mired in corruption and injustice. It wounds me to think that my own son is at the heart of it. A paper is a unique enterprise, Mr. Purser, with

166

a mission that does not exist in any other business. A good paper is the watchdog of a community, looking after its well-being. My late husband and I have always felt that there are things so important that we must report them even at cost to ourselves, whether in advertising, subscriptions, or acceptance.

"A city without a watchdog newspaper is a city in darkness. Bad things happen in the dark; when the light of truth shines upon these dark things, they usually stop. In this case, the justice system has been twisted to support the city government and fill the pockets of my son's political ring. I grieve it so much it's like a stone I carry in my heart.

"You've no doubt worked in many print shops and newspapers, both good and bad, caring and uncaring. Somewhere within you, Mr. Purser, you know that what my son's political ring is doing is evil and hurts innocent people, especially the drovers up from Texas. You know he's doing wrong and that victims suffer from this abuse."

She waited a moment, trying to read his face, trying to grasp what lay behind those rheumy blue eyes. But except for a small smirk pasted on his lips, she couldn't much fathom whether she was dealing with someone who still had a residual conscience or merely another of the world's apes.

"I would like to ask you to join the right side, Mr. Purser, as a matter of conscience."

"Oh, I'm already on the side of all good things, ma'am."

"What does that mean, Mr. Purser?"

"At your service, ma'am. We'll put this issue to bed in no time, and you needn't worry your head about it."

He had a deft way of being insolent.

"Then I take it you aren't interested in helping me?"

"Mr. Drum is very interested in maintaining a peaceful and prosperous town, and that is a splendid mission, worthy of any paper."

"Is that it?"

"At your service, Mrs. Drum. Why, we'll have your edition out early, and you'll get plenty of sleep. Shall I return to my labors now?"

"In a minute. How much does Marty pay you?"

"Why, the usual sixty cents per thousand, Mrs. Drum."

"And?"

"Oh, ah . . ." His eyes lit up. "A wee drink or two."

"And?"

"The restaurant . . . and his back room, which has a nice cot."

"Is that all?"

"His protection, too. As long as I'm in the fair metropolis of Opportunity, sampling its gorgeous delights, no harm shall befall me. A most gracious condition, I must say, for in all too many delightful burgs there is a mean gendarmerie, men who pick on gypsies like me."

"I'll beat the competition, Mr. Purser. One dollar a thousand ems for setting type, a boarding room quieter and more cheerful than that dive you're in now, an open account at the Prairie Café, and an open account at any saloon you may choose, other than the Lone Star. And if you're harassed by Spade Ball, I'll see to your bail and get you out. That's better than what Marty's offering you. All that for setting my stories and running my press under my direction."

He smiled blandly. "Oh, a capital offer, a most generous emolument, a true and noble proposition, Mrs. Drum."

"Well, then?"

"I shall take you up on it in a month. I'm committed for the duration, you see. A man cannot go back on his word, you know. You yourself wouldn't want me to violate my sacred oaths and promises. That would be a dastardly thing, and Mr. Martin Drum would be wrathful and vengeful. Yes, madam, in one month, immediately upon the end of the shipping season, when Mr. Drum releases me from my bound duty, I shall present myself unstained to you for employment."

She dismissed him with a nod. She had tried the high road, appealing to what good there might be in him, to no avail. Then she had tried a purely commercial approach, and that had failed, too. Now she would try another and lower road.

CHAPTER 21

Angie rarely descended to the Cellar Liquor Store except to sell advertising, but she always had liked its dwarf proprietor, Oscar Meineke, who filled the whole cramped place with his boisterous self.

"Ah, it's Miss Angie," he said from his perch on a stool. "Come for some elixir to tickle the tonsils or to peddle ads?"

"Elixir, Oscar."

"This is a rare day in Opportunity, you purchasing spirits."

She smiled. "Every semi-lady, like me, has the itch to tipple after the dishes are washed."

"I don't know your tastes, or there'd be a quart on the counter. By the time I see my regulars' shoes on that stair, I've got their choice off the shelf."

"Well, you can help me. What is the absolute finest, smoothest, most celebrated whiskey in your stock?"

"A gift?"

"Bribe. I imagine that's the word for it, Oscar."

"Well, there's the Tennessee, the Knoxville, aged in oak casks for seven years, a hundred proof, slides down like mead. A man sips it and swears he's with the archangels. Then there's the Kentucky, the Paducah, slightly less famous and but a bit livelier, to my taste, and many a gent prefers it. I just don't think any citizen of Kentucky knows how to distill good sour mash corn spirits the way they do in the Volunteer State. Also, the Paducah's ninety-six proof, a little less bombast when it purrs, but who's to know it? It's a lot cheaper, Angie. Four bits less per quart, and no one but a Vanderbilt would know the difference."

She stared at the bottles as he deposited them on the counter. "Which is the most famous?" she asked. "Fame is important. I want a label that's celebrated by every whiskey-drinking man in America. A legend, if there is such a thing."

"Oh, that settles it, Angie. The Knoxville. The wives of drunkards hate it. Widows despise it. Deserted children and orphans fear it. Preachers and temperance women revile it. Seduced maidens, the Odd Fellows, Knights of Columbus, the Brotherhood of the Protective Order of Elk, the Masons, and the Mormons hate it. Yet you'll find it in every gentlemen's club, every spa, every watering hole, every famous bordello from New Orleans to San Francisco . . ."

"Ah, how much would a drinking man require to turn a toilsome eve into a glowing one?"

"Oh, that varies with the gent's poundage and self-indulgence, but you'd better get two quarts anyway. One quart never suffices for True Believers."

"Wrap them up, Oscar!"

"Some advice, Miss Angie. If your purpose is wooing, stop at two stiff drinks. Three drinks and your dreams have wilted."

The gnome laughed nastily while she glared.

He deftly rolled the bottles into butcher paper and soon Angie had her two quarts. Her purse had been lightened by four dollars and sixty cents, but it was all for a good cause.

She felt slightly guilty, but argued that the end justified the means. It was dubious moral ground, but, after all, Purser had been given his chance to mend his ways, and even the opportunity to earn more than Marty was forking out, which he might have accepted if his soul had been purely commercial.

She arrived just as Aunt Gladys was snapping her parasol up and down, making sure it functioned.

"I'm done," Gladys said. She glared at Purser. "He wouldn't set my editorial."

"What did you say in it?"

"We're for prohibition, curfews, getting rid of riffraff, the end of gambling, and shutting down the houses of ill repute. The wages of sin is death."

"Ah . . ."

"I knew you'd oppose me, which is why I wrote it after you left." She sniffed. "It's hard to be a lonely beacon of light."

"Gladys, go home and eat supper. At about nine, come back here dressed in old clothes that won't be hurt by ink. You'll be needed to administer more medicine when the patient awakes. You will be our Clara Barton this evening."

Aunt Gladys pursed her lips into an astounding Oooo. Then she winked. "And if I do, will you print my editorial?"

"No, *The Outlook* isn't as virtuous as you, and I need the liquor advertising."

Aunt Gladys sulked her way out of the door, snapping her parasol.

Angie headed back to the shop with her two shining bottles of black-label Knoxville.

"Mr. Purser," she said. "After you finish the edition, you may have these as a token of my esteem. But mind, you must put the paper to bed first. I'm told that this is the finest sour-mash whiskey in the country."

She placed the two bottles on the composing stone where they gleamed seductively in the lamplight.

Mr. Purser drew himself up and stared. "Knoxville, Tennessee! Bless me, I didn't know such elixir existed in Opportunity. Do you truly know what this is? The Hercules and Michelangelo and Shakespeare and Leonardo of all whiskeys: The Genghis Khan of all sour mash! Never have I had more than a miserable sip of such as this! And to what honor may I ascribe this?"

"Why, to our future fruitful association, Mr. Purser. In one month, as you say, you'll be working for me. I'm thinking ahead. We've done a deal and these two quarts are my handshake on it."

"Ah. . . ." He smiled gently, fairies and angels and cherubim in his eyes.

"I'll be leaving now, Mr. Purser. We've a good edition. You make sure it's all properly proofed and handsome, then print it, and then you're free. Marty will want a clean edition just as much as I do. I'll see you anon."

She hated like hell to do it, but steeled herself to resist the caterwauling of her conscience. She made her way from the shop to the front office and out into the heat of the evening.

Maybe it wouldn't work. He was a canny old galoot who could down a whole bottle without a burp. He'd just help himself and put out the paper his own way. A sense of futility engulfed her, but she shook it off.

She dined at the Prairie Café instead of going to her cottage and propping her legs on the hassock as she usually did after a long day of walking and standing and typesetting.

She gulped a dreary swill of gray beef smothered in gravy and hastened into the twilight heat. Then she strolled slowly along Kansas Street, past her plant, glancing furtively into the grimy window at the man hunched over the composing bench far to the rear. She saw no evidence that her scheme had advanced. He had his type stick in hand, setting the last of the week's stories. She saw neither bottle nor glass.

She trudged home, disheartened, unhappy with the close, damp heat. All for nothing.

But wait.

A dreary hour later she threw a shawl around her shoulders and penetrated the night, steering away from the cowboy district by heading north at once to Kansas Street. Over on Lone Star Street, where Marty made his dubious living, piano chords honkied the dudes. She reached *The Outlook* in full dark and saw no one at the bench, though the overhead lamp burned. Maybe that was good. She let herself in.

He was sitting on the newsprint, the quart bottle in hand, filled with some interior gaiety. He laughed, smiled, blubbered, licked his chops, and listened to the spheres.

"Good evening, Mr. Purser. Are we done?"

"Why, it's the little lady. Thelittlelady . . ."

She saw in a glance that he was a-sail for the evening and that the front page remained half done.

"I'm glad you like the whiskey," she said, setting aside her shawl and donning her printing smock. She retrieved her notes from her desk and studied them briefly. There would not be time to handwrite the story first; only to compose it as she set the type. She was used to that, but such stories never seemed as good as those she had written and edited first.

"What is it thee be doing, madam?"

"I'm setting a story about the cowboys and justice, Mr. Purser."

"Ah . . ." he proclaimed sagely. "I know what that's about."

"Do you approve?"

He laughed.

She studied the notes and began. Time was flying.

"Large numbers of Texas drovers arriving in town are finding themselves in the court of Justice of the Peace Sid Wannamaker," she wrote. "They are being detained for no apparent reason other than to fatten the coffers of the city and of the town marshal and his minions."

She began recounting the stories she had acquired in the camp, dwelling on the details even though she needed to rush all this into print. Names, dates, charges, bail, amounts, detention records, losses, the behavior of the police, what was left in their pockets after their ordeal, if anything . . .

Mrs. Busby wandered in, observed Angie setting type under the green-shaded lamp and Fox Purser sitting on the newsprint enjoying himself.

"Ah, it's the old auntie," said Purser. "Inclined slightly toward virtue, but given to lapses, thank the Lord."

Aunt Gladys puffed up like an adder.

"Gladys, your task is to help Mr. Purser enjoy the evening. Later, you'll help me proofread this stuff and run the press."

"But Mrs. Drum —"

Angie never stopped setting. "Is it true that

you're a leader of the Temperance movement, Gladys?"

"Of course."

"And is it true that your lips have never tasted spirits?"

"Absolutely."

"And is it true that you'd rather roast in hell than to let spirits pass your lips?"

"You know me well, Mrs. Drum."

"Yes. And tonight, you'll do your duty even if you end up in hell?"

Mrs. Busby sighed. "There are larger callings," she said, a-tremble. "Mr. Purser, let us share that vile hooch you have in hand."

CHAPTER 22

They finished the press run at about one. The formidable Aunt Gladys not only soused Mr. Purser whenever his tongue wagged, but helped with the proofing and the printing.

Angie settled the last sheet on the stack to dry and straightened up wearily. Before her was an edition that would shake Opportunity. It contained two bedrock stories about municipal corruption, and Gladys's prussic acid-tinged editorial. Now it would be up to the town to decide whether to purge itself of its injustices. Or maybe the state. With the publication of this issue, the venal justice system would not escape the attention of the attorney general.

She felt proud and fulfilled. Oh, how sweet it was! Against all odds she had put out this telling edition. She had found the one crack in Marty's armor and slid through it.

The printer lay peacefully on the grimy floor, the half-drained quart of the lord of all bourbons clutched to his bosom like a relic of a saint. Earlier he had posed an unexpected problem when he slid into oblivion atop the stack of newsprint. But Angie and Gladys had rolled him off, watched him plummet to the planks without harm, and restored the quart bottle to his yearning hands.

"We're done, Aunt Gladys. Thank you for staying."

The woman pouted. "I've violated my oaths. I'm doomed," she said.

"Straight to perdition," Angie retorted tartly.

"Spirits have passed my lips."

"Fumes, if you ask me. You didn't sip enough of that stuff to fill a teaspoon."

"I'm dizzy and sick and nauseous, and you make sport of me."

"Absolutely schnockered," Angie said, enjoying Gladys's turpitude.

"Yes, to my everlasting shame."

"You're a fallen woman, Gladys."

Mrs. Busby blinked and pushed back tears while Angie wearily wiped down the old press.

"I did what you required of me," she said dolefully.

"I'm going to require one more thing," Angie said. "We've got to get this galoot out of here."

The women eyed the Bunyonesque printer.

"I shall wake him up," Gladys said.

She knelt over him. "Fox. Foxy, my fiendish friend, it's time for you to go home to your little beddy-bye."

Aunt Gladys prodded him decorously. The printer mumbled and resumed his snoring.

Angie decided on sterner measures; fetched a dipper full of water from the drinking pail and dashed it into Mr. Purser's serene mug.

"Ah! Ooh! A torrent! I'm drowning!" the printer said. His eyes opened and focused slowly.

"We're closing up, Mr. Purser."

He struggled to sit up, his wounded countenance surveying the gloomy corners of the shop and then the women.

"A fine evening," he said, discovering his bottle in hand.

"The Attila the Hun of whiskeys," Angie said.

"Is that so? I hadn't heard it."

The women helped him rise and steered him to the door. He stumbled into the night and promptly settled down on the front step, his bottle in hand.

That would have to do, Angie thought. Kansas Street was as good a place as any for tramp printers. She turned down the wick, shepherded the groaning Mrs. Busby into the night, and locked up carefully. She didn't want that galoot to slip in and ruin her edition.

"We'll see you in the morning, Mr. Purser," she said. Actually, she doubted she would see him again. Marty would give him the heave-ho the moment he saw the new issue. "Mrs. Busby, I'll walk you home."

Aunt Gladys didn't object. Angie left her at her rooming house swooning about her fall from grace, and trudged wearily home. At six she would be back at the plant, folding papers and readying them for her two delivery boys, Jackie and Aubrey. She wouldn't get much rest, but that didn't matter. Her joy had canceled her tiredness, and she was aglow.

She spent the remainder of that shining night in her chair wrapped in an afghan, her feet on the hassock, too exultant to sleep and too saddened by what she was doing to Marty to find peace.

Resolutely she met the dawn, downed some buttermilk, and hiked to the paper, wondering how she would get through this new day. Purser was gone. She let herself in, ran the papers through the folder, tied them in bundles for the boys, and quietly addressed her exchanges.

The youngsters showed up promptly at six-thirty and were soon scattering the edition on doorsteps and stoops and porches throughout Opportunity, in time for most people's breakfast. They would eat corruption with their kippers this morning. The thought gladdened her.

Promptly at eight, she trundled her exchange copies to the clapboard post office, which actually was a wing of Wilber's Mercantile, and waited for Horatio Bates to open up. He didn't arrive until eight-fifteen and let them both in.

"Your edition delayed me, Angie," he said. "I don't know how you did it, but congratulations."

Angie settled the exchange copies on his counter. "I did it by exploiting the weakness of almost all gypsy printers, Horatio, and I'm not proud of myself."

Bates laughed knowingly as he counted the

papers, licked stamps, collected her cash, and hauled the edition back to his sorting table.

"No one's going to show up for an hour. You come back here and tell me how you did it," he said.

Angie started to object, but then surrendered. Mrs. Busby would keep shop for her. "Well, Horatio, I did it by purchasing the best of all bourbons as a small gift for Mr. Purser."

"Ah! Pluck!"

"Design, Horatio, cold, cruel design. But before resorting to tricks I tried redemption, conscience, and wage competition."

"There's no redemption for printers, Angie. But lengthy penance can sometimes redeem a proofreader or editor."

She was in rare humor in spite of the tiredness that pierced to her bones, and it didn't take long to tell the postmaster the whole story, and Aunt Gladys's noble sacrifice of her loftiest ideals for the sake of something larger.

"What did Gladys think of spirits?"

Angie laughed. "Through the evening she compared them to turpentine, cod liver oil, creosote, red peppers, linseed oil, and garlic. About midway through she was smitten with a great mystery: how could drunkenness be so rampant when spirits taste so vile? If booze tasted like chocolate or Parker House rolls, she could understand the universal corruption. But she could not fathom how spirits could be a danger to anyone, even a child, since whiskey was the vilest concoction ever set before mortals. We'll see this morning how she resolves this conundrum."

The postmaster steepled his hands and turned grave. "Angie, you've struck hard at them, including your son. Don't suppose they'll take it lying down. Mark my words, they'll strike back, and maybe so hard that Marty can't bail you out. Ultimately, he can't control what the justice of the peace and the city marshal do to you."

She hadn't thought much about it. All she had hoped to do was cleanse a community far gone in venality. "I guess I'll have to endure whatever comes," she said. "I won't be the first editor to face the music. Sometimes the suffering is worth it, and this is one of those times."

"You're a brave woman, Angie. Editors have been shot for less."

She smiled.

"I'm not joking. Editors that upset someone's apple cart are targets."

"Horatio, don't be melodramatic."

The postmaster slipped into silence for a moment. Then, "They don't make many like you, Angie. Keep on fighting, and if you need help, I'll help any way I can. Postmasters have resources and contacts."

She nodded, stood, impulsively kissed the flabby man on the cheek, to his utter astonishment, and headed into a gorgeous late summer morning.

But at *The Outlook*, she discovered Marshal Spade Ball lounging on the stoop, waiting for her.

"Yes, Marshal?"

"Lies, Angie. I'm taking you in. Criminal libel. Felony warrant signed by Justice Wannamaker."

"Criminal libel?"

"You can't say things like that about public officials and get away with it, not under the laws of Kansas."

She drew herself erect. "Truth is the ultimate and perfect defense against libel, Mr. Ball. Star chamber trials happen to be illegal. Do you want it all out and on the court record?"

He snarled, grabbed her arm, and dragged her bodily toward the jail. She knew that she might be a long time getting out, and that when she did there might be no *Outlook* to publish anymore.

"Have you talked to Marty?"

"This ain't Marty's business."

"I was afraid of that. So it's you and Sid."

"And most of Opportunity. It's the end of the road for you, Angie."

"To you, Mr. Ball, I'm Mrs. Drum." She decided to walk proudly and met his stride so he no longer was dragging her. "You may not address me familiarly."

He laughed.

They reached the jailhouse. He tossed her into the stinking cell, and she watched the steel-strap door clang shut.

CHAPTER 23

When Marty Drum trotted downstairs to his saloon, he discovered that the world wasn't his oyster after all. There, before his eyes, was *The Outlook*, and the music of its front page was not his choice for reveille.

He read it studiously, poking it for weakness, and he found none. His mother had done her work well. The story was taut, understated, not a bit inflammatory, grounded in interviews — and damning. She had nailed him. His world tottered. He did not know how much of the damage he could reverse, but he would try.

He began by reprimanding his daytime barkeep, Gordy West, at the cherrywood bar. "Dammit, I've told you twenty times, whenever there's an earthquake, wake me up."

West shrugged. "So that's an earthquake?"

"What does it take? Mount Vesuvius? Now I've lost time."

West polished glass beer mugs diligently, holding them to the light and rubbing away fingerprints.

"Where's that printer?" Marty asked.

West gestured with a thumb.

Marty stormed down a short hall, out the

back door, and then into the rotten little closet that Purser called home.

"You're fired. Get out."

Purser stared up from his cot, innocent-eyed, and blinked.

"I told you to keep the lid on. What did she do, bribe you?"

"I remained your obedient and humble servant to the end, sir."

Marty spotted the half-drained brown bottle of Knoxville booze and understood. His mother was wise to the ways of tramp printers and had found a way to put her own edition out. He plucked up the bottle.

"But, Your Honor, that's a gift from your sainted mother!"

"Now it's mine. Call it payment of your rent. Be out of here in ten minutes, or I'll throw you out."

Purser yawned, baring randomly rooted yellow teeth and two serrated ridges of pink gum. "A fine way to treat a man. That's why I'm an anarchist. Abolish law. Abolish property. Abolish government. Abolish employers. All right then, all right."

The printer swung his hairy, white legs over the edge of the cot. Marty didn't wait around.

Back in the saloon, he barked an order to West.

"Throw him out in ten minutes," he said, and headed for the street.

Angie had outfoxed him. He hated to do it,

but he needed that paper to undo her mischief. First, a retraction. Then a story that contradicted Angie's. And an editorial that would say *The Outlook* stood firmly behind the mayor and the court. God, how did he get into this mess? He despised his mother, even while admiring her. What kind of feeling was that? Like hopping around on a checkerboard, red squares and black.

The implications were clear to him as he strode swiftly through the noontime tide on the clay streets. For a few painful weeks, he would run *The Outlook*, write the stories and set the type. There wasn't anyone else in town who could set type, and he couldn't rely on Angie.

He wasn't sure what to do with his mother, but he would think of something. One thing was certain: she would not set foot in that building again. He would force her out.

Ah! Retirement. Angie was about to retire. And her dutiful son would make sure she was comfortable.

He stormed into the front office on Kansas Street and discovered only that peculiar, purple-plumed, broad-beamed woman at hand.

"Where's my mother?"

Aunt Gladys lifted a silver lorgnette, eyed him imperiously, and turned her dowager hump toward him.

"I asked, where is my old lady?"

"I'm sure you already know where your mother is, Mr. Drum. It is beneath my dignity to consign you to nether regions, and I am trying hard not to think it for the sake of Christian charity, but you tax me."

"I would like a direct and businesslike answer."

"Ask the marshal," she said.

He should have thought of Ball. The man was obviously detaining his mother for the fiendish crime of writing something unsavory about him. The marshal was solid ivory between the ears and in need of direction. He sighed.

"You're discharged. This paper is closed."

He waited. She refused to budge.

"I said, vamoose."

"You don't own this paper, Mr. Drum."

"Out!"

Then she did the astonishing. She grabbed her pink parasol and began to whack him soundly, arm and limb.

He glanced around wildly. It would not be good for the mayor of Opportunity to be caught under siege from a rotund dowager. But no one was noticing. He snatched the parasol and ripped it from her soft white hand. Then he propelled her through the door with a firm hand to the elbow.

She swiftly recovered her dignity, huffed, and brushed off her skirts. "Mr. Drum," she said softly, "your triumph is just as ephemeral as butterfly wings."

He realized he didn't have a key, but he flipped the CLOSED sign and shut the doors. Then he thought better of it, slid back inside, and emptied the case boxes onto the floor with a fine, satisfying clatter.

There would be no furtive editions of *The Outlook*.

Then he wished he hadn't done that. He could have used the paper to give voice to his administration. So he retrieved the case boxes, set them on a bench, and left, ashamed of his own confusion and impulsiveness. It would take hours to sort the pied type.

He found Ball ruling his empire, all right, and his mother sitting quietly in the cell. Her gaze daggered into him.

"I've been expecting you," Ball said. "She's in for criminal libel and sedition. She's libeled the constabulary and Sid's court. I was just about to take her across the street for the bail."

"And Sid's going to try her?"

"Who better?" Ball snapped.

Marty began laughing. He wheezed so derisively that Ball took offense.

"What's the matter with you, Drum?"

"Unlock her, Spade."

"The hell I will."

"Spade, you're the best man in the West when it comes to keeping the peace. You can whip ten Texans one-handed. But you'd better learn a few statutes before you find yourself on the wrong side of those bars yourself."

The marshal glowered.

"Can you read? Can you write? Do your numbers?"

Ball's eyes glowed like hot coals.

"What is the meaning of sedition?"

"Printing stuff!"

"Has it occurred to you that if Sid's a plaintiff, he can't try the case? Has it dawned on you that Sid's municipal court enforces city ordinances, not state laws? This would have to be tried in a district court. And has it dawned on you that when that happens, your little pocket-lining party's over? You'll spend a few years wishing you could see daylight without all them iron bars between your innocent orbs and the sky. Now let her go."

"Never. She'll just publish more sedition."

"I've already seen to that."

"That's what you said last time, Drum. She stays right there."

Marty Drum eyed his mother. "We'll go palaver with Sid," he said, motioning the marshal out. She was all ears, and he wasn't going to clothespin any more laundry if he could help it.

They crossed Kansas Street and found the unshaven justice of the peace snoozing in his chair behind the bench.

Marty had always thought Wannamaker resembled a monkey. He had a simian face, with big flap-ears and slicked back jet hair. He had arrived in Opportunity just about the time the town was forming its first government and asked to become the justice of the peace. He had a pair of lawbooks in arm and a quick tongue with legal Latin. It didn't take long for

Marty to discover that the cockney knew less about law than he did and that the Londoner had little grasp of the American court system.

But Wannamaker had proved useful. He meticulously turned over to the city every cent he fined the Texans, and even some of the court costs. But those court costs had been so high, often exceeding the fine, that he'd fattened on them along with the city. He had evoked the ire of the Texas cowboys, but they couldn't do anything about it. Between Spade Ball and Sid Wannamaker, Opportunity didn't lack funds to run itself.

That trip across Kansas Street was all Marty needed to conclude that he'd better bail out his mother, and fast. Already, Gladys Busby must be henning the news around town, and Marty could see only big trouble in that.

"Look at this contumely!" Wannamaker snarled, shaking the paper. "She's in contempt of court."

"Criminal libel," said Ball.

"Neither," said Marty. "She's not in contempt unless she's been disorderly in court, or she's violated a court order."

Wannamaker waggled a bent finger. "I've ordered her a dozen times not to write up court business."

"It's her legal right, Sid. And a court order has to be a written and dated command. Have you filed one? Is one in your court record?"

"No, but I'll do it right now."

"Let her go, Sid. You can't charge her with a thing. She's not broke; she can afford a lawyer, and if wind of this reaches superior courts, you're in the rendering kettle."

The monkey stroked his ears doubtfully.

"Then drunk and disorderly conduct!"

Drum laughed. "Forget it, Sid. I'll take care of this. She won't publish another edition."

Wannamaker snickered.

"I'm going to talk to Magnus Garrity. He'll front for me. Buy her out. Retire her. Meanwhile, she won't even get into the plant. I'll see to it. It's no trick to buy two padlocks."

Wannamaker glowered. "I want her hide. She published this stuff."

"Is it true?"

"Not a word of it."

"Then sue her for libel, bribe some witnesses, and go to court up in Topeka."

Wannamaker subsided fast.

Marty knew he had won. He held out his hand, and Spade Ball dropped the jail key into it.

A few minutes later, Marty unlocked his mother and told her to wait for him in her house. She sailed past them and into the sunlight, a small, courageous, great-hearted woman who had impeached the whole ring.

CHAPTER 24

Angie was free. Even those two hours in that cell had been a month too long. Quite apart from the foulness, what she would always remember was her utter helplessness.

Her son accompanied her along Kansas Street.

"Thank you for freeing me. Now I wish to go to work," she said.

"No, the paper's closed."

"You have no right."

For once Marty didn't smile. "Yes, in fact, I do. Public safety. That inflammatory issue's heading south with Texans who'll share it with everyone coming up the Chisholm. I've the safety of this town to consider. I won't have any more such issues stirring up those boneheads.

"A Texas cowboy's a strange critter, Ma. About one-quarter gentled, three-quarters wild. Just like those longhorns they drive up here. Mean and well armed and dangerous. It doesn't take much to set them off."

"I have business at my paper. Subscribers. Stories. Advertisers. All of them depending on me. It's mine, not yours."

"It's padlocked. I had a man bolt the hasps

this morning, and now it's locked." He pointed. "See?"

She saw the padlocks as they reached her whitewashed building. Her one and only, very own, legitimate son-of-a-bitch was doing this.

"*The Outlook* won't miss an issue," he intoned velvetly. "There'll be one out next week. Ads, stories, and all. I can set type as fast as you can. You'll like it. So will I."

"It won't be *The Outlook*. It'll be some painted whore of a paper. I know what'll be in that issue, and it won't be truth, and my paper will never be quite the same. Papers have souls."

He laughed uneasily. "I just sprung you from jail," he said, as if that was exculpatory.

"Yes," she said, "and wonder why. If you want to get rid of me, that's the right place to park me." Was it his filial devotion? She held her peace. Maybe there were questions a mother should never ask.

They reached her weathered cottage, which had started out butter-colored, but had surrendered to the sun long before. She did not invite him in. "I suppose I'm a prisoner here," she said.

"No. But I'd like you to think about retirement. Selling *The Outlook*. You've worked hard, and now you deserve some rest and security."

"Marty Drum, you get out of here. I've never been so . . . so ashamed of you . . ."

She swallowed the rest and corked away her feelings.

He smiled that big, bright, ingratiating smile he had always worn when he was manipulating her.

"You think about it," he said.

"I intend to publish, Marty."

"Forget it," he said, and waved his good-bye.

She entered her house, a free woman. At least Marty had done that for her, whatever his motive.

Her modest cottage had never been grand, but she and Gideon had filled it with love and surrounded it with lavender lilacs, and within it they imbibed food for their souls as well as bodies. She had always believed — until now — that Marty had learnt integrity there as well as the shop.

These were sad thoughts and did nothing to lift the oppression that gripped her.

Still, it did no good to moon. She remembered Horatio Bates's offer to help publish out of town. Maybe next week there would be two editions: the real *Outlook*, clean through and through, and Marty's slut.

She washed, wanting to scrape away the foulness of that cell from her face and hands. Especially her hands. She poured tepid water into the basin and scrubbed them furiously with yellow soap and then dabbed them dry. They remained ink stained, but ink was honorable and the sign of her vocation.

She knew exactly what she should do: buy a pad of paper and some pencils and sit down and write. A story begged to be told. And she should wire the *Abilene News* about doing an out-of-town edition, if only a two-page sheet. She should put on the brass knuckles and come out swinging.

But she found herself sagging into her Morris chair. That trip to jail had drained her. This feud with her own son, the child of her loins, cut her to the quick. She could scarcely sort out the grief, love, hurt, anger, fear and tenderness that vied for her heart. Thus did an hour crawl by, and then two more, and then a rap jolted her out of her chair and set her heart to tripping.

The man whose knuckles tattooed her flimsy door was one who had never before visited her cottage, and who lived on the other and higher side of Opportunity. Magnus Garrity stood on the worn stoop, his black bowler in hand, his gray-shot hair unloosed by the Kansas wind.

She marveled that a bank president would venture so far from his own precincts.

"Yes, Mr. Garrity?"

"Ah, madam, you look fetching this beautiful summer's day. May I have the pleasure of your company for a short while? I bear good tidings, yes tidings of great joy."

She eyed him sourly. "Ah, are you announcing a birth in a manger?"

He laughed and waited for her to motion him in. She did, leading him into her homey parlor, which was scarcely larger than his shining desk at the bank. He settled himself gingerly — she suspected hemorrhoids — and sighed as the brown horsehair sofa surrendered. She was curious as to whether it would survive for more than five minutes of Garrity.

He proved to be a great hat-rotator, and his bowler turned like a clock gear.

"Would you like tea?" she asked. "Sun tea, cooling in my root cellar?"

"Why later, perhaps, to celebrate."

It was plain that Garrity wasn't a man to speak directly, so she settled down to endure some resistance-softening small talk, which proceeded from cattle to weather to drought to green-bellied flies.

"I head a small group of businessmen, all established and prominent citizens of Opportunity," he said, shifting down into business like a gravedigger who's cut through the soft sod and into the hard clay.

She knew, suddenly, what this would be about, but merely smiled.

"We've noted that your splendid paper's profitable and doing very well. Its circulation keeps rising; it wins respect everywhere. We did some quick measuring and find that fully sixty percent of your space is devoted to display ads, and another five to ten percent goes to cards and classifieds. Very impressive.

"We took the liberty of totting up some figures, madam, and discovered in your paper a lucrative business with a sterling future as Opportunity grows into a county seat — it's coming, you

know. We've lined up the right men in the legislature."

He paused pregnantly to let all that filter
home. "Mrs. Drum, we're prepared to make a
generous offer. We've talked to some knowl-
edgeable men. They tell us that your building,
equipment, supplies, Washington press, the job
press, fonts, folder, goodwill, existing subscriptions, and all the rest, are worth about six thousand dollars. We're prepared to offer quite a bit
more."

"How much more?"

"Twelve thousand in all, lock, stock, and
barrel."

"Lock, stock, and barrel alludes to a rifle, I
believe."

"Ah, just a figure of speech. The point is, this
is a dream come true for you. Money enough to
live comfortably in your little cottage. Or travel.
Or head for warmer climes. Or visit relatives. I
think the bank could arrange the sale of this cottage for you and add to your nest egg. At long
last, a life of hard work rewarded."

"Who are the principals?"

"Oh, I'm not at liberty to say. Not yet."

"Is my son involved?"

"I can't name them, Mrs. Drum."

"All right, if you can't name them, I'll reverse
the question. Is it correct that Marty is not one
of them?"

His eyes lit merrily. "I'm not used to trading
witticisms with sharp editors. At any rate, that's

the offer and there's but one proviso: that you do not begin a competitive paper or any other type of literature within a hundred mile radius of Opportunity. We wouldn't want our investment jeopardized."

"How much of that twelve thousand are you putting in, Mr. Garrity?"

"Oh, that's confidential."

"Anything at all?"

"Oh, yes, I will be a principal and a director."

"You're fronting for Marty. He has a lot of gold in his vault after cleaning out Bo Waggoner."

The bowler stopped rotating.

"I think this has less to do with my future and my comfort than with shutting me up. Is that correct?" she pressed.

"Oh, I can see how you could draw such inferences, Mrs. Drum, but we're all looking at *The Outlook* as a rare and choice investment opportunity that should yield us twenty percent or more a year, a tidy sum divided among the partners."

"And I imagine, since I've done so well, you'd like me to stay on until you can hire a printer and editor and maybe an ad salesman?"

"Oh, no, there'd be no need of that. We've already lined up the required personnel."

"Sure, it's Marty Drum. Well, that's one way to stop the exposure of his shakedown ring, which is really why you're here."

"Twelve thousand dollars, Mrs. Drum, is a once-in-a-lifetime opportunity."

"Yes, it is," she said. "I will sleep on it."

CHAPTER 25

Angie loved the quiet of the night. That's when she could think tender thoughts. Newspapers were not known to nurture tenderness. She sat in the ticking darkness, her white shawl drawn around her, her feet on the hassock, just letting time and thought glide freely by.

She had been wrestling with remorse this evening. Images of her dear departed Gideon had haunted her, especially those of his last years when he was steadily drinking himself to death. She hated ardent spirits for what they had done to a man who had no other weakness and a boundless passion for goodness and truth.

She had defeated Mr. Purser with drink. True, he was destroying her paper, but two wrongs didn't make a right. Marty had swiftly sent the tramp printer down the road where he would wield the type stick in some other little burg until the itch to move along caught him. She could almost sense Gideon standing there in the soft dark, disapproving.

"You shouldn't have used a man's weakness, Angie . . ."

"I had to, Gideon . . ."

Unlike many women whose loved ones had

been destroyed by drink, she didn't despise spirits or saloons. Neither did she have much sympathy for the Temperance movement, which was trying to impose its will on everyone. She had always believed that spirits could be a blessing or a curse and that it was up to each person to decide whether to be a slave to a vice or master of himself.

Poor Mrs. Busby, caught in purple sin. She had violated her temperance oath because Angie had wanted her to. Two people had suffered at Angie's hands just so that she could get her paper out. What sort of woman was she to permit that?

Was it worth the effort? Odd that no one in Opportunity had spoken to her about that edition of the paper. No businessman, no woman, not one of the clerks or professional people. Was it possible that not one soul in Opportunity except Angie cared about ordinary justice for ordinary people? Was it possible that everyone in town was so used to living without property taxes that justice didn't matter? Were they all willing to profit from theft, as long as the robbery involved strangers?

She had always trusted the public to respond to a scandal and demand reform. She had that Jeffersonian belief in the goodness of the American yeomanry. But now she doubted that she and paper and the heroic measures she had taken would move the community one inch. Maybe that was good enough reason to quit. No one cared.

And yet, she knew some people cared. Horatio Bates cared. The town's businesses hadn't stopped advertising. Maybe they were all just waiting to see whether she triumphed or her son did.

Every sash in the cottage had been lifted, and she felt the night breezes eddy around her in the velvet darkness.

She had a decision to make, and she had been putting it off, not even wanting to consider it. Twelve thousand simoleons was more than she had ever seen in her life.

She and Gideon had scraped by, printing on used equipment, buying used fonts, struggling year in and year out to keep afloat and at the same time raise a family. She thought of her three dead children, but not much. That was too painful a memory to revisit.

Twelve thousand dollars. Why, that was more than twice the value of her little paper. The false-front building was worth twenty-five hundred at the most. The old Hoe handpress, the job press, folder, fonts and other equipment came to fifteen hundred and some. Her subscriptions and goodwill and accounts receivable didn't amount to much. It was a bribe, this twelve thousand. It was Marty's gold, probably what he had taken from that poor Texas stockman who had killed himself.

If she sold, Opportunity would slide into darkness. She wouldn't want to live in a town like that. Every town needed a good newspaper.

She was nearly alone now; that was plain. Opportunity shunned her more than ever. No one much cared about the cowboys, those brawling sunbaked summer visitors whose sojourn was always marked with mayhem.

And yet someone should defend them, just because it was the right thing to do. They needed defending. They were scarcely literate and not well versed in law and courts and justice and appeals and bails and jury trials. How many of them had ever asked Sid Wannamaker for a jury trial? Just one that she knew of.

Someone had to stand up for their rights. Angie decided it might as well be her. Even if she were the only one in Opportunity to stand up for justice, she would do so because it was right and nothing else mattered. There were times when she refused to be practical or prudent, times that required a lonely recklessness and an indomitable will.

She knew then that she would not sell out, not even if they raised the stakes still higher. Not even if they tried everything they could think of to shut her down. She did have one ally, the postmaster, and that might be the key. If she were to print her editions elsewhere, Horatio could funnel her copy out, and funnel galley proofs and printed editions in, and no one in Opportunity could stop the United States mail.

Tomorrow she would talk to him.

At last she went to bed, her mind made up.

The next morning she felt different, all itchy and keen to start. A burden had lifted from her. No amount of money for *The Outlook* would ever tempt her again. She dressed swiftly in a speckled green calico and decided to catch Horatio at his home. She puzzled that in her mind, trying to remember where the old bumbler lived, and finally remembered he had rented rooms above Wilber's Mercantile, the only two-story building on Kansas Street.

So that's where she walked before the egg-yolk sun slid over the northeastern horizon. She found the recessed side door at the corner mercantile, climbed the noisy gray stairs, and studied the doors. There were two. The upstairs had been sliced into two apartments. She didn't know which was Horatio's and tried to find some sign that might help her. Just when she was nerving herself to knock on one door, the other opened, and she beheld a stranger.

"Is this Mr. Bates's room?" she gestured toward the other door.

The man nodded and closed his door.

It took a few long minutes before Horatio Bates opened to her, peering around the slightly opened door to conceal from her view whatever he was or wasn't wearing. He blinked.

"You? This is not a proper hour. I'm not properly attired, and the condition of my rooms mortifies me."

"I need you, Mr. Bates."

He sighed. "Wait while I robe myself and sluice down the place and eject a stack of old *Outlooks* from my cracked-leather chair, salvaged from a dump years ago, and scrape off the geologic strata."

She stood quietly in the gloom. The city had not stirred, and she heard no wagons rumbling by, no team, no stagecoach, no voices or foot traffic. Only a murky silence.

After an eternity, the door creaked open, and she beheld the postmaster in a shabby blue robe, his few remaining hairs slightly slicked back, and gray stacks of books and magazines and papers teetering on every grubby table and shelf and scattered in heaps on the floor.

"I don't entertain," he said.

"Consider this business. I need advice and help."

"That I will offer in short order. I've started a fire in the range and my one culinary skill, making coffee, will be put to the test. It is good to see you, looking so fresh and bright . . . and virtuous."

He was studying her.

"I could get rich," she said, perching delicately on a battered black chair. "I could make twelve thousand dollars by saying one word: Yes. I thought about it all night."

The postmaster stared.

She told him about Magnus Garrity's visit and all the things she didn't find out, such as the names of those proposing to buy her out. She told him what she believed *The Outlook* was really worth.

"And?"

"Gideon's ghost must have been beside me. I will not do it. A town without a good paper is a town without a beacon. If I don't fight for justice, no one will. So, Horatio . . ."

"That was a courageous decision."

"Oh, it wasn't a decision at all. I just do what I must."

"You could have taken the money."

"Horatio, I'm not as virtuous as you think. There's a lot of good living and kicking up my heels in that much money."

"You are a rare woman, Angie."

"Medium done and tender, if you ask me. Now I've got to publish out of town, and that's where you come in. All I'm asking, Horatio, is your confidence and discretion."

"I'll work with you, Angie."

"Good. Maybe it'll only be one issue, but it'll sure as hell howl about what's happened to me."

He fussed and sniffed, as he always did when she uttered unladylike tropes.

They visited a while more. Angie disagreed with Bates about one thing: his coffee was not a culinary achievement. There were men better off trenchering in restaurants, and he was one.

"Angela, you are a gallant woman," he said at the door.

The next step was the portentous one.

She had to track down Magnus Garrity, who

wasn't in his office. She found him tilted at a forty-five degree angle in the tonsorial parlor next door and braved her way into that masculine enclave. The barber, Cyrus Canute, was deep into the shave and haircut, and two other duffers were awaiting their turn. Garrity, well lathered and trapped in the barber's chair under the apron, squinted at her while Canute was scraping bristle off his left jaw.

"Magnus," she said. "If you won't spill the beans, there isn't much I can do. We're stuck tighter than a champagne cork. I want the paper in the right hands, you know. The next owner must be someone who truly cares about justice in Opportunity. Someone who isn't afraid to tackle city hall or the justice of the peace if need be."

Garrity eyed her, but said nothing and didn't move a muscle for fear of the straightedge scraping over his jugular.

She laughed. "I rarely get to talk to some man who can't reply," she said.

He glared. The barber paused, blade in the air, as if to let him speak, but Garrity chose not to.

"So, you see, Magnus, I can't even consider your offer until I know who's lusting for my little rag and what it is they believe in. Twelve thousand is about three times the value of what I have there; so either someone is pretty dumb about values, or he's trying to shut me up. You said you're one of the buyers. So which is it,

Magnus? Are you just dumb, or are you trying to stitch my tonsils?"

They all stared at her. She laughed. This day a good yarn about that wild Angie invading male precincts again would float around town.

CHAPTER 26

Marty Drum didn't like to set type, but he was the only person in Opportunity, apart from his mother, who could do it. So the next edition of *The Outlook* was up to him.

His mother irked him. She had caused him more headaches in recent weeks than he was willing to tolerate. He didn't want to hurt her. That's why he offered to buy her out at a generous price. He could afford it, thanks to the killing he had made from Bo Waggoner's reckless night of gambling in the Lone Star. But now she had turned that down, too, according to Magnus Garrity.

The mayor nurtured a sulphurous mood. That morning he had cut himself with his straightedge and now wore a plaster on his jaw. He was a city official and a saloon operator, not some paid type slinger. He had spent bitter hours sorting the pied type, and now his brimfire anger leaked into his work, and he was constantly revising to keep his lead story from sounding vindictive.

The task was simply to undo his mother's reportage. He artfully quoted Spade Ball at length about the violent, dangerous, drunk, thieving, and disorderly conduct of the cowboys.

He quoted Sid Wannamaker about the modest fines in comparison to the gravity of the charges against the Texans and explained that the cowboys who spoon-fed his mother those tales were simply vengeful and their nonsense was not worth listening to. Let Spade and Sid find out what they had said when they read the paper. The thought amused him.

As for the city funding its government with the fines, he could point to a simple reality: its income came from the licensing of saloons, gambling tables, and houses of assignation, and the mayor himself was paying a stiff fee for his saloon and gambling tables.

Any other moneys, including those extracted by the justice court, were simply a minor increment, and in any case supplied income only a few weeks of the year. In fact, the cost of law enforcement during the cattle shipping season ran so high, with the need for extra part-time deputy marshals, that the city police court fines didn't cover the true costs of keeping the unruly Texans orderly.

Thus did Marty set his story, keeping it plausible, authoritative and understated, knowing that it would largely undo everything Angie had written.

From the moment he had taken over Angie's paper, he had concerned himself with the running of it. He had posted the city clerk, Dinky Smothers, in the front office to keep books and handle subscriptions and classifieds, while Spade Ball and his deputies were rounding up the display ads. Drum's Ring needed a mouthpiece, and he intended to keep this one afloat.

He was setting a graph commending the police work of Spade Ball when his mother walked in, glanced at Dinky, and headed straight toward Marty.

He braced himself. This time he wasn't going to take her whining, and he wasn't even going to stand still.

"Marty, this is mine. My building. Take off that smock and leave at once."

"I told you not to come here. Do I have to throw you out?"

"I won't sell the paper to you. Not ever."

"Who says I'm trying to buy it?"

Her gaze was enough to melt wax. "You're setting a story that will contradict mine. Is it truthful?"

He laughed. "More than yours."

Her stare daggered into him.

He set down the type stick, irked at the delay. He didn't like to hang around a newspaper. He hated even to set foot in one. But she needed some counsel.

"Don't try to print an edition out of town," he said. "It won't be distributed here. It won't get far from the post office or the train station. It won't be read. You'll just waste time and money."

"Thank you for warning me. I will make other

plans to spread the news."

He should have been glad to hear it, but he sensed menace in her voice.

"Such as?"

"Not your business, Marty."

"You could move to someplace nice. Kansas City, maybe. And have enough to be comfortable."

"After thirty years, you still don't know me. I believe in things. I'll never sell out to you or your ring. Not ever."

He grinned. "Never say never. How about a higher offer? I hear Magnus is preparing to offer more. Here's a secret I'll share with you. Insist on twenty thousand. That's what the buyers are prepared to offer. You can get it if you hold out. Twenty . . . thousand . . . smackers."

He melted no ice in her glacial eyes.

"I won't be bribed," she said.

"Do you know how much twenty thousand is?"

"Yes, it's just about four times the value of my paper. Do you think that's my price? Are my beliefs worth just that? Do I value twenty thousand more than honor and truth and justice?"

He shrugged. "What's your price, then?"

She didn't respond, and he reddened.

"I'm busy," he said. "I'm doing a story pointing out that the city's income is almost entirely from licenses, including the ones I pay for the saloon and gaming tables. You wish to challenge that?"

"And what is the income of your ring? Fines from unjust law enforcement."

He picked up the type stick and began work again. She glared, and then, catlike, grabbed the galley tray and threw it to the floor. The story scattered into thousands of fragments.

"Hey!" he snarled.

In a rage, he clamped her arms and hustled her through the front doors.

"Don't come in here. I'll throw you out, and you won't be standing when you land."

"Marty . . ." she said, softly. There was such sadness in her voice.

For a moment that final rebuke haunted him.

He stormed back in, furious. Another three hours lost. An hour to sort the pied type; two to reset the story. He plucked up the type and threw it viciously into the case boxes, volcanic heat flowing through him. He wished he had thrashed her. Why the hell had he been born to some witch like Angie?

The clerk was staring.

Marty worked bitterly, cleaning up and then resetting, certain that the second time around the story would be less persuasive than his original. He couldn't recall all the facets of the original. He couldn't even remember the words he had put in Spade Ball's mouth, or how he had quoted Justice of the Peace Wannamaker.

Spade Ball was the next to show up, watching quietly while Marty set type and fumed.

"Your ma pop you in the jaw?" he asked.

"Shaving. Used up half a styptic pencil stopping it. You get some advertising?"

"It's easy," Ball said. "I go into a place, and I say I'm selling space ads, and they say okay, marshal, sort of nervous, and I say I'm increasing the space they're buying by fifty percent, and they say hip hooray, and I add it up and make them sign the advertising order, and then I ask them what to put in the ad, and pretty soon *The Outlook* has a big fat ad. I want twenty percent, Marty."

"You got it."

"Is your mother gonna sell?"

"Maybe if the price goes up."

"To what?"

"I don't know. I could start a rival paper cheaper, that's all I know."

"Well, why not? Drive her out of business."

"She's still my mother."

"That ain't bothered you much."

"It don't bother me at all. I just want to go easy if I can, but I'll get rough if I have to. Trouble is, she won't quit. She's likely to try printing one out of town. From now on, you and your deputies watch the express shipments and the mail, and don't forget the stages coming in. I don't think she can do it. It'd take awhile to send copy out and get a paper back. But you watch.

"And one more thing. Watch the newsboys. If they're pitching papers at houses, first you pinch them, take what they carry in their delivery bags, and then you just whip back and get every copy off every porch and bring 'em in here. We'll burn 'em. Don't make a ruckus, and don't beat up on those boys. Just watch 'em. You want to tell your deputies that or should I?"

Spade Ball grinned. "Arresting newsboys," he said. "Styptic that one."

"I told Angie she'd never distribute a paper in this town, so I don't think she'll try. She knew I meant it. And another thing. Keep an eye on Addison McCoy. He's her biggest backer. Horatio Bates is another, but he's harmless."

Ball nodded easily.

"One thing more. If my mother catches a train somewhere, don't stop her. If she goes somewhere, maybe that's good. But get Jimmy Babcock at the train station to tell you where she's going. I want to know."

Ball nodded.

"You all set for Hash Brown?"

"I'm not afraid of Hash Brown."

"Thirty or forty armed men, Spade."

"If he tries to tree this town, there'll be fifty armed men on the roofs with rifles and scatter-guns, and a few other surprises. Like a posse at the bridge collecting their sidearms. I plan to enforce the firearms ordinances around here."

"They can borrow weapons. Or buy them."

"Not rifles. How many cowboys carry rifles?"

"All right. But Opportunity is counting on you to keep it safe."

Ball nodded again. Marty liked that nod. Of

all the marshals in the West, Ball was the top man; the deadliest, the most courageous, the most effective. And every Texas drover riding north knew it.

Ball left. Marty grimly tackled the story that would salvage his administration. But now the words wouldn't come. When his mother had pitched his story to the floor, she had shattered more than a column of type.

Angrily he stalked the shop, type stick in hand, heaping word upon word and coming up with air. Nothing made sense. He could not recover the lead sentence from wherever it had fled.

He drifted to the front office and peered into the sunlit street. It seemed so bright out there, so dark within. The ink. The ink, yes, that was it. The ink had stained everything black. All pressrooms looked like that, grimy and bleak.

He grew aware of his mother's presence everywhere. On a coat tree hung her mauve cloche hat and a creamy knit shawl. He espied her black slippers under her desk. She must have pulled off her shoes whenever she could, weary from a day's standing at a composing desk.

Everywhere he discovered order and chaos that neatly matched her own. Each issue of her paper had been pressed into an archival binder. But the exchange papers lay haphazardly on a table, some opened, some untouched. Her two printing smocks, ink stained and worn to tatters, hung from pegs on the wall.

A sepia tintype of Gideon, his father, stood in a small wire-gold frame at her desk. Gideon looked almost as young as Marty was now. Odd, Marty thought, that he had scarcely noticed that image before. He decided he looked more like Angie than Gideon. He had his mother's blood.

Dinky was staring at him.

"Go back to city hall, Dinky," Marty said.

The young clerk hastened out the door and into the sun.

Marty stood alone in his mother's newspaper, listening to the whitewashed clapboard building groan in the heat. It had never been just a newspaper for her, but a grail from which she sipped communion wine each day.

He knew that every second he stood there in Angie's paper he would suffer. His plan to commandeer the paper and turn it to his ends wouldn't work; the very walls of Angie's paper mocked him.

Slowly he retreated back to the shop, turned down the wicks, pulled off his printer's apron, washed his hands in the vitreous china bowl, and headed outside. At the door he slid his padlock through the hasp and locked it.

There would be no issue at all next Thursday.

But once he had reached the street and the warm sun, he felt better.

CHAPTER 27

Addison McCoy crossed the bridge over the Little Arkansas with a tight grip on the reins because his fleet thoroughbred trembled at the hollow thunder of its hoofs on the planks. He was keeping a tight rein on his own fears as well.

The new herd south of town was probably that of Loran Jakes, out of Victoria County, deep in southern Texas. That's what he had heard. And if Jakes was arriving from that far south, Hash Brown couldn't be far behind.

The thoroughbred was McCoy's trump. It would outrun any cow pony up from Texas. The height of the shipping season had passed, and fewer herds were showing up. It would all be over in a few days. McCoy's own tautness somehow transmitted itself to his mount, and the bay thoroughbred seemed jittery, ready to bolt, spooking at things unfathomed by the livestock broker. The horse was working up a sweat on its withers and stifles, even though the weather had turned mild.

He reached down and laid a hand on the neck of the animal under its mane, calming it and himself. The bay would wear itself out in five miles if it jittered along like that. An hour later he reached the knob from which he liked to survey the country. It gave him only a fifty-foot advantage, but that was all he needed. He reined the bay and pulled out his little brass spyglass.

Yes, there, off to the southwest, rested a goodly herd, a dark mass upon the tawny veldt. He could even make out the chuck wagon and the tiny forms of men around it. If that was indeed Loran Jakes, the man would soon be riding to Opportunity to deal.

McCoy collapsed his spyglass, tucked it into his saddlebag, and rode toward the herd. When he reached the outermost beeves, he saw at once that this was Jakes's outfit, the J-Cross. After that he rode in with more confidence.

Jakes, on horse, rode out to meet him.

"Come to bid on your herd, Loran. Nice looking outfit."

Jakes grunted. He sat weary in the saddle, stocky, dark, and bald as an egg under that wide-brimmed sunshade.

"Maybe I'll sell, maybe not, Addison. I figure you know why."

"You've been hearing plenty, I'll wager."

"For five hundred miles we've been hearing plenty. There's not an outfit that didn't get whomped out of trail wages and then some by Drum's Ring. If you can't guarantee our safety, we're just gonna plow on up to Abilene and put 'em on the Kansas and Pacific."

"No, I can't guarantee that Spade Ball won't

219

lay a hand on your boys, but I can tell you how to keep your cash. There's an art to it. If you do what I suggest, you can ship here. And I'll make you a better price than you'll get in Abilene because the grass's plumb gone between here and there."

Jakes sighed. "That puts my tail in a crack."

McCoy felt his mount lash at blueflies with its tail. It stood restlessly, not wanting to be reined down.

"Here's what I'll do, Loran. We'll cut a deal, and I'll pay you any way you want. Ball usually leaves the trail bosses alone because he wants you back next year. But not always. He's got no habits. You can get a letter of credit from the bank, and there's nothing he can do about that.

"But what I'm suggesting is, your men don't need to carry much cash in the cowboy district. Dole out two dollars apiece and keep the rest of their trail wage in camp. This afternoon set up a bar tab in any resort you choose and let 'em drink it up. Tomorrow they can safely buy whatever they want by daylight on Kansas Street. But tonight keep the cash out of their hands."

"They won't like that. And what happens if they can't make bail?"

"If there's anything Spade Ball hates, it's feeding a cell full of broke cowboys at his own expense. The city doesn't pay him for that."

"Other outfits done this before?"

"Set up a tab? No, but I just thought it might work."

"The boys'll grumble. They've been waiting for months to blow their wages on Lone Star Street, with cash in their britches, too." Jakes's cow pony shifted under him, as restless as McCoy's thoroughbred. "If we agree on a price, I'll try it. But if my boys don't get out of that calaboose the next morning, you're going to have to make bail."

"I'm willing to risk that."

"We hate this. Every man in my outfit's gunning for Ball."

"Not wise. He's deadly, and never more than when he's outnumbered. He patrols with a double-barreled scattergun now."

"Who says they'll fight fair? They're ready to backshoot the sonofabitch."

"They'll end up in the Kansas pen, Loran."

Jakes squinted. "We figure Ball's signed his own death warrant. If it ain't us, it'll be Hash Brown. He's four days back of us, McCoy. Just four days. And he's been collecting grievances all the way north like they were fifty-dollar poker chips. He's got so much revenge to do he's more interested in that than shipping beef."

"How many men?"

"Twenty with the first herd, sixteen with the second. And when they hit, there won't be no Opportunity left. And the first to go'll be Marty Drum, Sid Wannamaker, and Spade Ball and his deputies. And they's talking about you, too. Which is why I'd just as soon get my herd sold, dole out pay today, and get out of here. You got cattle cars coming?"

"Season's slowing down. I'm getting cars now. You want to ship tomorrow? I can do it. I can load well over a thousand a day."

Jakes pondered that. "What's your price?"

"I'll need to walk the herd first."

"No, no time for that. I want this sold today and loaded tomorrow."

McCoy reined the thoroughbred through clumps of cattle, mixed stuff, and came to a swift conclusion. These were good animals, and he could sell them for twenty-four dollars in KC.

"Twenty-one fifty a head, Loran, after a tally. Anything born this year doesn't count. Plus shipping."

Jakes veered the cow pony close and held out a big paw, and they shook.

"What's your estimate?" McCoy asked.

"Oh, we started with twenty-seven ninety, and lost about a hundred ten. Some trouble at Red River, mostly."

"They look better than I thought for this time of year."

"Some rain in the Nations greened things up again."

"We'll tally at the pens. It's easier."

"Suits me. I just want to get the hell out of here with my pay before Opportunity disappears and you along with it."

"I'll be ready for you."

McCoy set his thoroughbred into an easy rocking chair lope and crossed the bridge in less than an hour. He headed straight for the station with two wires in mind. One would request stock cars by tomorrow; the other, in coded language, would trigger something he had worked out weeks earlier with the Santa Fe. He had asked for all of their railroad dicks to be on hand when Hash Brown showed up. The railroad had a dozen tough customers, some out of Hell's Kitchen. They promised eight when he needed, and he asked that they be ready when he sent a coded message three days hence.

His next stop was the bank. He prepared a letter of credit that would require only that he fill out the blanks and sign it. And, in addition, he collected a thousand dollars in small-denomination greenbacks; payroll cash. He stuffed these into his satchel and locked them into his little strongbox on the second floor of the whitewashed Atchison, Topeka and Santa Fe Railroad station.

He hiked to the jail to tell Ball of the arrival of a herd, as he always did. Ball wasn't around, but Eddie Farrar was.

"Herd's coming this afternoon, Eddie." He paused. "Watch your back. I've warned you."

"Whose?"

"J-Cross from Victoria, Texas. Loran Jakes."

"He ain't what we're bothering about."

"Well, I've warned you just the same."

His next stop was the Lone Star Saloon. He

stepped from sunlight into gloom, and let his eyes adjust. The place had an eerie quality by day, like any old bar with cracks in the boards that let blinding light into darkness. It took some getting used to.

"Where's Drum?" he asked the barkeep.

The man pointed up.

McCoy hiked around to the side door, up the noisy wooden stairs, and knocked on a door already open to let breezes through.

"McCoy," Drum said. The man looked haunted.

"I've a herd coming in. It's the last one before Hash Brown. You treat those boys right and maybe they'll tell Brown you've let up."

Drum stared, his face a blank.

"Marty, you listen. I heard threats on your life out in that camp today. Your life and others."

"Who made them?"

"The J-Cross outfit from Victoria, Texas. And they were mostly talking about Hash Brown, who's four days out."

"We're ready. Not a cowboy crosses the bridge wearing a sidearm."

"You've been warned. Maybe you can still fix it. Send these J-Cross boys south with good news and some refunds to spread around down there."

Drum laughed shortly. "Fix it, McCoy? I guess that tells me what I want to know about you."

"I'm not in your ring, Drum."

"Then you'll have a little trouble doing business next year."

"You've been warned. Three times now."

McCoy swung on his heel and banged down the long stairs into the clean street.

He had one other destination, over on the other side of town: *The Outlook.* But when he got there he found padlocks on the doors and darkness within. What had happened?

He circumnavigated the dead building, rattling the front and rear doors, learning nothing. Not that he needed to have this story spelled out. It was plain enough.

Ten minutes later he knocked on Angie's door, and she opened to him.

"What happened, Angie?"

"Won't you come in? Marty locked me out."

He didn't ask her for reasons as he followed her into the homely parlor with the antimacassars on the horsehair furniture.

"Angie, Hash Brown's four days out. His outfit's going to revenge every Texan that Marty's ring ever gypped. There's murder in the air, and Marty's on the list. I just got all this from Loran Jakes of the J-Cross. They're coming in right now. . . .

"Maybe it's too late, Angie, but I've tried to reason with Marty. I still think that if the town treats this outfit well, there's a chance that Brown'll stick to business."

"Oh my God. Tell me about Hash Brown, Addison."

McCoy did, sparing Angie nothing. In the menacing personage of that Confederate veteran boiled all the revenge and hatred and malice of a thousand Texas drovers; a force that might level Opportunity.

She sighed. "That does it. I'll put out an edition, warning people. This city's in danger."

"How?"

"I bought a hacksaw," she said. "And a padlock of my own. I'll get in the rear door. I'll work without lamps. No one will know that I'm in there. Maybe I can save Opportunity."

"Why, Angie?"

"That's what newspapers are for, Addison."

"Angie, be careful what you say."

"It is not a time for carefulness," she said.

CHAPTER 28

Angie kept watch in the alley while Addison McCoy sawed through Marty's padlock. It seemed to take forever, but at last he swung the padlock off the hasp.

"Good luck, Angie," he said. "You're the finest woman I've ever known."

She stared at him, sensing more than a compliment in his voice. He was a widower. She found herself smiling.

"There's no way to put this padlock on the hasp and make it look like the building's locked if you're inside," he said.

"I don't think they'll notice."

"You look tired," he said. "You all right?"

"Yes," she said. "A little worn out."

"All right, Angie," he said, doffing his wide-brimmed hat.

She paused at the rear door, watching that fine and upright man slip out of sight. Then she entered.

Darkness cloaked the shop. She felt like a thief breaking into her own building. She edged forward toward the two windows on Kansas Street, trying to avoid the glare. She wondered whether people could see in. She certainly could see everything on Kansas Street, the busiest artery in Opportunity. She had no way to curtain herself, but maybe that was all right. All she needed, really, was something to block the view through the doorway into the back shop, and she did have that.

She hung newsprint from that inner doorway. Her sheets didn't reach the floor, but they didn't have to. She would be able to work by day, but not by night. The only risk of exposure would be running the press, which clanked and shuddered with every imprint.

She would have to set type without lighting a lamp, but she couldn't help that. Marty had missed a trick. He should have made off with the type sticks. Impulsively, she hid one in her desk drawer.

Then she donned her printing smock and studied the advertising orders. Marty had coerced her advertisers into buying more space than they needed. She would undo that. In all cases she would run updated versions of last week's ads, which would save time.

She dreaded setting the type. If she set type and produced this fugitive issue of *The Outlook*, she would change Opportunity forever, hurt Marty, and maybe ruin her own enterprise. Yet, she had to. She gripped the type stick as if it were an instrument of salvation, something holy. She wondered if she could perform this ritual when her mind tumbled and turned, the things she wanted to say skittering like a hundred aggies on a playground.

She had never tackled a harder story. What should she call Marty? What should she call herself? How could she write without turning it into a family feud? Dear God, how could she accuse her own son of anything at all?

She felt faint and ached to retreat out that rear door and flee this place. What had summoned her here? Duty? Revenge? No, something more abstract — and loftier — than that. Justice.

She stared at the dimly lit case boxes, hoping the letters were in their right pockets, that some other vexation wasn't about to pounce.

"The Drum Ring attempted to close this newspaper last Thursday," she wrote, plucking letters out of the case boxes. She examined the first line by taking it to the rear window. It was fine. The font was intact and properly sorted.

"*The Outlook* had published a comprehensive account of abuses by our police and court system, which funnels fines into the city administration as well as private pockets. The response of the administration was to throw the editor and proprietor of *The Outlook* out of her own building and padlock it. That not only violated her freedom of speech, and the right of a press to publish, but numerous other civil rights and liberties as well. By denying her access to her own property, the Drum Ring was engaged in criminal conduct . . ."

She hated that word. She hadn't meant to call

Marty a criminal. Anything else would be better.

And yet, he was a criminal. She let it stand. She slid the lines off of her type stick and into the galley tray one by one, adding leading to keep the lines from crowding one another. The story grew. It wouldn't be a long one. What was there to report?

She remembered to include Marty's response: he was shutting her down for the sake of public safety. "The mayor claimed that *The Outlook*'s stories were inflaming the minds of the Texas drovers and endangering Opportunity."

And then she quoted herself. "The editor of this paper pointed out that the Texas drovers had long since turned bitter as the result of city-condoned graft that emptied their pockets. *The Outlook* has done nothing to provoke public disturbance, and, indeed, its editorial opinion, expressing the hope that city officials would stop their unjust practices and return ill-gotten fines, may be the single most important step toward preserving the peace."

She set type for an hour, numbing her heart and mind to the pain she was feeling, and the pain that Marty would feel. The pain might do him good. Nothing else had deterred him.

The story grew to ten, twelve, fourteen inches, and then suddenly she was done. The light hadn't changed. The shop remained dim; the sun had merely rotated west. Not a knock, not a rattle of the doorknob, had disturbed the eerie quiet.

She paused awhile, slipped into the front office and peered discreetly out the window. A beer wagon rumbled by, the oaken kegs resting in a row. Twice people passed her window, and she ducked to the side in the nick of time. Deputy Farrar strolled the opposite side of the street, past the milliner and the apothecary shop and the soda parlor.

She returned to her work, screened by the newsprint in the shop doorway. The other important story would cover the imminent arrival of Hash Brown. She couldn't verify it, so she would simply quote Addison McCoy as her source. And she would carefully say that it was rumor and speculation, but prudent readers should take their own measures. She'd be damned if she would terrify a whole town with some half-baked, unverified yarn about the Great Avenger.

Still . . .

Hash Brown, she wrote, would probably be the last of the Texas cattlemen to take herds up the Chisholm this year. He was expected any day, with two herds a day apart, probably totaling forty-five hundred beeves. He ranched in extreme southern Texas, in Jim Wells and Duval counties, and was famed for the swift expansion of his herds and the haste with which other cattlemen sold out to him.

She wrote carefully, avoiding the sensational, but making sure that any reader would grasp what might lie ahead. That story taxed her mind more than the one about her son, which had drained her of every feeling in her heart. But she persevered.

She turned next to an editorial. This would be her opinion about her own son, naked to the world. She dreaded that editorial, but her own stern sense of rectitude would not be placated until she did.

"The Drum Ring should be thrown out of office," she began. "And that includes the entire police force as well as Justice of the Peace Wannamaker. The ring survives only because of the venality of those citizens who think getting a free ride instead of paying taxes justifies the cruelty, theft, and injustice of the current system.

"There are those who might argue that the current shipping season is about over, the injustices will soon cease, and therefore nothing needs immediate attention. They are wrong. This evil system should be destroyed at once, with a stake driven through its heart. A thousand men bilked of their wages cry for reform and justice. This must be dealt with immediately.

"The only responsible act that the Drum Ring can do now is to abandon office and return their ill-gotten gains. That alone might spare its members prosecution by state officers. Nothing else will. The public disorder here is well known to state officials, and it is only a matter of time before the corruption of this city will be cut out of the body politic of Kansas.

"This paper, and this editor, wish to state un-equivocally that this abuse of public office must cease and desist, and if the citizens of this town are loathe to remove the malefactors, others at the county and state levels will do so, with potentially harmful results to this town . . ."

She continued in that hard, uncompromising vein, aware of the deepening gloom, the hushed mean dark that crept into the printing shop. When she finished the editorial and proofed it, she realized the darkness was really within her. She was saying this about her own boy, and every word had cost a tear.

The dinner hour came and went, but she proofread until dusk defeated her. When she could see no more, she carried the heavy galley trays into a closet, set them on the floor, and covered them artfully with an old tarpaulin. Then she removed the newsprint from the shop doorframe and finally let herself out the alley door in soft, warm darkness, using her own padlock instead of Marty's to lock up. Tomorrow, she would finish the lead stories, set whatever news had been pushed under the front door by various church secretaries and other people, redo the ads, and print in the afternoon.

She wondered how she might distribute the paper. Marty had warned her that his deputies would be on the prowl, ready to pounce on her newsboys. She decided not to summon her boys at all, but to distribute it herself, plucking thin papers from the canvas shopping bag she often carried. She also decided to leave free copies with a few merchants she trusted, in lieu of having her newsboy hawk the papers on the corner of Kansas and First Streets.

She stepped into her own dark cottage too weary to eat and settled into her chair and hassock, filled with premonitions of doom.

CHAPTER 29

Fever. Her body had betrayed her. Or maybe she had betrayed her body. All she knew was that she was riveted to the chair where she had spent a miserable night.

She eyed the gray pre-dawn light and knew she had work to do. This day, of all days in her life as a newswoman and editor, she had to put out a paper.

She dreaded rising from the chair. Dreaded even throwing off the shawl that covered her. She knew she was not just sick, but bone-weary after weeks of being torn to pieces by her conscience and her love for her son.

She felt hot and thirsty, and nothing in her didn't hurt.

She was being asked to do too much. No woman could do what she was asked to do. Asked by whom? God? Maybe her own stern rectitude, her vision of a good commonwealth governed by honorable men. Maybe the things she had imbibed not only as a girl in a strict family, but also from Gideon, that beautiful man with a single, fatal flaw.

"Oh, Marty . . ." Did her son have any idea what he was doing to his mother? Any regret or even tenderness? Did he see her as anything other than some obstacle or annoyance, keeping his ring from dominating the town for years to come?

She didn't know. Her usual insight into him failed her. She only knew that this pale and fateful morning, when Opportunity hung in the balance, she was fevered and desperate.

She willed herself out of the chair, poured a dipper of water into a tumbler, and drank. She didn't feel like eating. She tried to wash her face, but wanted only to crawl into her small bed. She could not do that.

Her body burned and yet she felt chill. She wrapped the shawl tightly around herself and tried a tentative step or two. Somewhere within her she must discover the courage and strength to do what she must this day. She walked, wanting not to. She stepped outside into soft and gentle air with the scent of the prairies upon it. The sun had not yet lapped the eastern horizon.

She made her slow way through a hushed town, her nostrils engulfed of the acrid smell of cattle down in the railroad pens and the harsher scent of cookfire in the stoves of many kitchens.

She could use filler material to help things along. She would do the ads, make up the pages, and stuff holes with junk. But running that press, a task that taxed her to her limits even when she felt well, loomed as darkly as a nightmare in her mind.

She reached the alley door of her building, saw no one, and found the key to her own padlock in her pocket. It released the lock with a soft click, and she let herself into the gloomy shop. It was still too dark to set type, but she could make up pages and stuff holes with filler.

That dawn she toiled slowly, resisting the need to curl up on the floor. She completed pages two and three, and finally four and one, setting display type for the headlines. She could see that the August day was a fine one. Hot as always, but fresh and spirited.

She proofread, readied the old Washington acorn press, and began printing. The clank of the platen deafened her, and she believed she would swiftly be discovered. She raged at the thought of being caught like a criminal in her own building printing her own newspaper. By the time she had printed ten copies on one side, she had reached the edge of her strength, so she rested quietly.

She spotted Deputy Farrar walking by and froze. But he didn't pause. She willed herself to stand up and print some more, and finally fell into a slow rhythm, her fever regulating the muscles she had to employ.

She blamed her own stubbornness for her fever. Everything she did was tearing her to bits. But then she stopped assailing herself. It was truer to think that everything that Marty did was rending her life apart.

Somehow, little by little, she printed a hundred sheets on both sides. She knew she could do no more. Her fever raged within her and everything hurt. The pain in her head, behind her eyes, maddened her.

The hundred sheets would take care of half of her subscribers and leave nothing for her newsboys to hawk or the exchanges. But it would be a published edition. And she could print more tomorrow, or whenever she found strength, and get them to the post office and her advertisers.

She was slumping in her chair when she noticed Deputy Farrar peering into the window. But then he drifted away, and she supposed she was safe enough for the moment. But she couldn't be sure. Marty might walk in at any time, for any purpose.

For a while she curled on the floor of the shop, too exhausted to begin folding. But at last she struggled to her feet and began running the sheets through the folder and into a neat pile of printed papers.

She marveled that she had done all that. Now she would have to distribute them, another herculean task, beginning with the homes on the outskirts where the police didn't patrol, and working inward to the business district. She had a nice canvas tote she could use, and no one would stop her.

But it would take several trips, and she worried that the copies she left in the plant might be seized. She couldn't help that. She didn't even know how she could walk the newsboys' route and place so many copies on so many porches or stoops.

She stuffed thirty thin papers into her tote, slipped into the alley, and locked up again with her own padlock. Then she trudged north across Kansas Street and into quieter precincts. One by one the papers reached their destinations while her bag grew light upon her shoulder. She repeated the whole cycle, distributing another thirty or so. No one noticed or cared.

Maybe it was all for nothing.

By mid-afternoon she had distributed all she had printed, save for two archival copies. She locked up and stumbled to her cottage, falling into her bed without even unlacing her hightop shoes. Never had a soft bed felt so blessed.

She slipped into oblivion and didn't awake until much later. When she did grow aware, she realized she lay in a darkness that felt comfortable and safe. She had no idea how long she had lain abed. She felt cooler and realized her fever had abated. She sat up and unlaced her shoes. She stood, stretched, and discovered that the weariness had not left her even if the fever had.

She fumbled toward the kitchen, scratched a stove lucifer and lit the coal oil lamp. She carried that into the parlor to examine the seven-day clock ticking there. Four-twelve in the morning. She had slept a dozen hours.

She returned to her room, slid out of her clothing, and into a soft clean nightgown and her old blue robe. A peace had settled within her, and it matched the hush of the night. For as long as the war within her had raged, it had fevered her. For as long as her love of Marty had jousted with her need to make the world right, the armies contesting for her soul and heart had bled her of strength and health, polluting her springs, tearing up her grass, ripping her flowers from her gardens. Now that had passed, and she felt whole.

Her sense of goodness had won. Most women would have said that her love of goodness had triumphed over her love for Marty. Most mothers would have stood by their sons, at all cost, in all ways, without questioning what they were doing. For most women, unconditional love of the child of their loins mattered most. But not for Angie. She would do Marty no favor by standing beside him while he inflicted hardship and injustice on innocent men, nor would she help him by averting her gaze when she saw him and his ring do terrible things to innocent people.

She had loved him and still loved him, and she regarded her public exposure of his twisted ways not as betrayal, but as a mother's ultimate and most profound love. For there could be no reform, no growth, no improvement in her son unless he faced the consequences of his greed and injustice. And it had fallen to her to raise the mirror before him.

She knew then that she had been a good

mother. A great peace befell her, and she sensed that her divided self had become whole, and that the broken parts of her heart had stopped warring, and that she could sleep and be healed now.

Tomorrow, if she was well enough, she would visit Marty. She would listen to his bitterness, if indeed he wished to talk to her, and she would reply, gently, that in everything she had been the best of mothers, and that the truest loyalty was not blind, but offered gentle rebuke, and that the truest love was not inhibiting, but encouraged growth in one's beloved. No matter whether Marty was ready to hear such things, she would say them to him.

She found herself curious about the impact of her edition. No one had come banging on her door that evening or night. No constables, no businessmen, no reform-minded women, and not Marty. It was as if all her brutal work, demanding more from her sick body than it could give, had been for nothing.

And yet, tomorrow might tell another tale. Maybe by tomorrow she would learn whether Opportunity lay in contentment, ready to let an unjust court system pay its municipal freight, or whether men and women of conscience would rise up and cleanse the Aegean Stables.

She turned down the wick until the flame blued and the faint scent of smoke drifted into the air. She stood at the window, gazing on the eternal stars, which hung like verities in a world of chaos.

She returned to her bed content and was soon asleep, the healing force of a clear conscience comforting her. When she did startle awake again, she found the morning well advanced, and that the sharp rapping on the door had summoned her back to the world.

CHAPTER 30

She discovered Magnus Garrity at her door and started to shut it.

"I won't sell out, not ever," she said.

"Wait! May I talk for a moment?"

She stared at the banker, who stood hat in hand on her porch. She nodded and let him in, tightening her blue wrapper to her throat and feeling indecorous.

He perched delicately on the edge of the horsehair chair.

"That was a fine and thoughtful issue," he said.

She nodded, still driving the fog out of her head.

"Perhaps the best thing that ever happened to Opportunity."

She listened hard now. This was not the same bank president who had knocked on her door with other ideas in mind.

"Mrs. Drum . . ."

He looked uncomfortable, and she didn't help him. She wanted this interview to end so she could go back to bed.

"Up until last evening, I truly believed that your son's administration was good for Opportunity. By shifting taxes away from our struggling new businesses in a frontier town, he offered us a chance to prosper, the magic touch . . ."

She nodded, feeling her guard drop a little.

"I hadn't thought much about injustice. About this whole business of hauling innocent Texas boys into our court and cleaning out their pockets. And neither had others. Oh, we all knew about it, but somehow it was a joke, a comical, slick practice. A way to stick those Texans with some of our own burdens.

"I . . . well . . . I just wanted to thank you. That's what I came here for. And to tell you I'm quietly organizing an informal coalition for change. There are some merchants who see eye to eye with me. You know, a banker's in a unique position. I decided I could do much."

"What?" she asked, bluntly.

"That's the question. Wait until the election next spring, or seek help from higher courts and the state attorney general."

"Which do you think is best?"

"Well, ah, that's what I'm here about."

"Every moment this injustice continues, Opportunity will suffer. I am talking about the suffering in our hearts. We may all get rich, but we will still be tortured."

"Marty's your son . . ."

"Marty's suffering exceeds all of ours."

"You really feel that drastic measures —"

"Mr. Garrity, for days that very question tore me to pieces. Even now I'm recovering from a fever. But then, as I put out that issue, sneaking into my own building like some thief, I came to a clear vision, and my suffering ceased. I love my boy, and *because* I love him, I would like to see whatever will bring him remorse, so that he may reach toward a new and better manhood."

Garrity stared, and when he spoke it was so quietly she could barely hear him. "You are a magnificent woman, Mrs. Drum."

She sighed. "This is the first sign that my efforts accomplished anything. Up until this moment, I just didn't know. I thought maybe the entire town approved of this . . . corruption."

"I could name twenty good men who hate it."

"And they never spoke up."

He stared out the window. "We were all fence-sitters. We also feared retaliation. Marty's made some things pretty clear. Support his ring or suffer some financial problems. He never quite said what he had in mind, but I wouldn't like Spade Ball hovering around my bank, intimidating customers."

"And now you're willing to take the risk?"

"Yes. We're very late. No one knows what this Hash Brown will do, though I think the whole thing's overblown. Spade Ball's organized some sort of militia. He'll put men up on the roofs, as if that would stop some veterans of the war bent on trouble. And I know that Addison McCoy's arranged to bring in some railroad detectives. Believe me, those are some tough customers, used to dealing with work gangs, thieves on passenger trains, express car robbers, pickpockets, and assorted malefactors. But I don't know. . . . Do you really believe that we can stave off Brown with some promises of reform?"

"No, not promises. But I think he might be willing to help the city return illegally gotten cash to Texas cowboys . . . if we asked him to."

Garrity smiled grimly. "I fear Hash Brown delights in darker plans, including the ruin of this town. He's rumored to be a pure devil. Seething with violence."

"You're probably right."

"For the moment, I'd just as soon not reveal our committee of vigilance to the public."

"Vigilance?"

"We didn't know what else to call it."

"Vigilantes hang people without trials."

"It was a poor choice of words."

Her pulse quickened. "If all my effort to address the evil here were to result in the hanging of my son, without a trial, you would be the death of me, Magnus."

"I understand. But there are some who are talking like that. Hang Spade Ball. Hang Wannamaker and . . ."

Angie felt sick. "I've struggled for reform, not revenge, Magnus! Reform! I don't want to hear one more word about vigilance committees."

He shrugged. "All right, Angie."

"Who's in this . . . this cabal?"

"Billy de Vere —"

"De Vere? He's the last one I'd expect."

"You're right, Angie. He backed the ring until a few days ago. You know what? He got scared. You know why? Because angry cowboys threatened to kill him. They rode into town, put up their cow ponies in his livery stable, and then the cowboys couldn't pay him because Spade and Sid Wannamaker had cleaned their pockets.

"When Billy threatened to keep their horses until they came up with the feed money, they got mad. It suddenly dawned on Billy that a lot of cowboys were ready to tear the town apart, including his stable. He came to me. He said he was afraid and sick of this whole mess."

"Who else?"

"Ed Wilber. He said his sales are down because the ring's siphoning off everything the cowboys earned. He said last year he sold more shirts and boots."

"Who else?"

"Joe Pflug. He said he had never heard such bitter talk when the cowboys brought their plugs in for new shoes. It scared him plenty. He said there's murder in the air, and if the cowboys ever busted loose, the town would be drenched in blood."

She got the names of several others, all merchants who discovered that the ring was wrecking their summer business with the Texans.

"Magnus, isn't there one person in that group who's against the ring simply on principle? Because it's unjust to treat innocent people that way? Because it's wrong?"

"No, Angie, I don't know of a soul. That's an abstract idea, you know. Most people take a commercial view of things."

"Then I've failed. For weeks I've written about the wrongness, the injustice, the venality of it, and they don't care about that. About the vision of a good commonweal. Magnus, there's hardly a person in Opportunity . . ."

"There's one, Angie. Me. You reached me."

"There's more, Magnus, Gladys Busby, my assistant. And Horatio. If there aren't any others, I guess I'll just move away. What good is a newspaper if there's no one with understanding?"

He sat quietly a moment. "We're calling ourselves The Committee of Ten, Angie. I'd like to buy some space in your next paper. I don't know what we'll say just yet. But I mean to put grafters on notice."

"Do you think Marty would even care, Magnus?"

"Yes. I plan to sign my name. Let him know that the town's only banker has drawn a line in the sand."

She smiled at last.

Garrity excused himself awkwardly, and she tried to get more sleep, but it eluded her. In any case, she knew she would receive a visit soon, so she combed her hair and then dressed, weary as she was.

She wasn't surprised when Marty appeared an hour later, knocking briefly before letting himself in. He had always done that, and she said nothing.

"You broke in," he said.

"Into my paper," she retorted.

"What did Garrity want?" he asked. He had that childhood smile pasted on his face again.

"So you've been watching me now."

"You warrant watching. What did he want?"

"We talked about my paper and how it had affected his thinking."

"And?"

"And what he's going to do about it."

He waited for her to spill more beans, but she simply shut up.

"You're ruining me. Your own son."

"You're ruining yourself, Marty. If I hadn't exposed your graft, someone else would have, someone less kind and quicker to see the worst in you. There's still time to pull back."

"Back from what? I've given this town the best deal it's ever had. That's my political base. People know how to add, and when they add up what I'm giving them, they'll hardly wait to vote for me."

She didn't want to go into all that again, so she just stared quietly from her Morris chair, a comfortable yellow afghan over her legs.

"It's not everyone whose ma turns against him," he said, an edge in his voice.

"I've never turned against you, Marty. Only against some of your deeds. I've wept for you. I've just told Magnus that I've struggled for reform and not vigilante justice."

Marty stopped smiling. "Vigilantes?"

She nodded.

"After me?"

She didn't move a muscle.

"What've I done?" he asked.

"Stabbed your own conscience in the back," she said.

CHAPTER 31

The time had come. Addison McCoy had heard from several men riding the Chisholm that Hash Brown's first herd would reach the bedding grounds south of town that afternoon. The second herd would pull up south of Opportunity the next day.

McCoy didn't really want to ride out there. Maybe he would never return. That was a real possibility. But he was the only livestock broker left in Opportunity. His two rivals had fled, not wanting anything to do with the notorious Texan and his henchmen.

Still, Brown had cattle to sell. Brown had been months on the trail from far southern Texas and would be eager to sell. Maybe even flexible. And his cattle would be in poor shape. This deep into August, there would be no grass left on the trail or on the bedding grounds, and every day Brown delayed, the heavier would be his losses.

McCoy set aside his impulse to flee as something unworthy of a real man. He would ride out there, do business if he could, and broker the deal. Only if Brown chose to be totally unreasonable, guaranteeing McCoy a loss, would

McCoy walk away from it. If he could.

He peered about him. Opportunity squatted tightly on the bank of the Little Arkansas in a fierce summer's sun, awaiting its fate. Odd how people seemed to hurry on the streets, eager to be indoors, as if flimsy doors and glass panes would protect them from a ruthless army.

The first step was to wire the Santa Fe. They promised him the railroad dicks on a twelve-hour notice. They would be arriving from east and west before sundown. He rattled down the stairway from his office on the second floor, plucked up a yellow flimsy, and wrote a single code word. Then he handed it to the day telegrapher, Norris Thwaite.

"Send it now, Norris. Code it for every wire office on the line, immediate response requested."

"Just one word? 'Blue'?"

"Blue," McCoy affirmed.

"Must have deep and mysterious meanings, Addison."

He ignored the remark. "I want confirmation that it was sent and received."

McCoy waited while the telegrapher hunched over the handsome brass and walnut key and tapped the message. A moment later the key began tapping, and Thwaite scribbled an acknowledgment.

"Red. That's all it says."

"That's all I need, Norris."

"It'd sure be nice if you said what this is all

about. Don't you trust a telegraph man who's never divulged one deal, not one, to any of your rivals?"

"Sure do."

Thwaite glared, waiting.

"I summoned the cavalry," McCoy said. "Four troops of the Seventh, led by the ghost of Colonel Custer."

"Blast it, McCoy."

"Now send another. You know the drill. I want every empty cattle car on the line. There's twenty-three here now. I need more fast. As many dropped off today as possible. Fifty tomorrow, and the same the next two days."

"I'll get 'em, Mr. McCoy. Hash Brown's coming, right?"

"Keep that shotgun under your counter loaded," McCoy said.

The telegrapher stared.

McCoy stepped into the sun and directed his feet toward Billy de Vere's livery barn, even though his feet wanted to go anywhere else. McCoy was shocked by his own cowardice. He, a veteran officer of the federal army, wanted to run. But he didn't run, and wouldn't, and maybe that was why he had ended up a brevet captain.

He stepped into the low gloom and spotted Billy at the rear of the aisle, raking away manure.

"Saddle up the bay, Billy. The time's come."

De Vere paused. "Brown?"

"Brown."

"You think there's going to be trouble?"

"I'm going to go out of my way to nip it in the bud, Billy."

The hostler vanished into the corrals at the rear of the barn, bridle in hand, and minutes later returned with the big thoroughbred.

"You plan to outrun 'em?"

"No. I'd be shot before I got fifty yards away."

De Vere brushed down the animal, slid a saddle pad over its back, lifted McCoy's old McClellan saddle on board, cinched it, and handed the reins to McCoy.

"You reckon those cowboys'll be putting up their horses here?"

"Your guess is as good as mine, Billy."

"Well, I don't want trouble. You tell 'em old Billy, he likes Texicans, and they'll get free lodging in this horse hotel. You think that'll do it?"

"They know you've been part of Drum's Ring, Billy."

"But I quit. Total, complete, and final."

"You're on Garrity's little committee?"

"I sure am."

"You part of Spade Ball's little militia?"

"I was, but I'm backing out of that, too. I'm just a peaceable old liveryman."

"Might be way too late, Billy."

The skinny hostler glowered.

McCoy turned the small steel stirrup, stuck his boot into it, and swung up. The McClellan was little more than a pancake compared to the heavy stock saddles favored in the West. But it lightened the load a horse carried. He clipped a canteen to the saddle and pushed his notebook and pencil into the small saddle bag. He would go unarmed.

He rode out of the barn, ducking his head at the front door, and turned the eager bay south toward the bridge. The worst of the summer heat had passed, and the air was dryer now. The breezes playful rather than dehydrating.

The bridge rattled underneath him, and then he turned the bay toward the nubbin a few miles ahead where he customarily glassed the bedding grounds. How many times had he done the same thing? How many years had he gone looking for the herds? Why was this time different?

He lifted the bay into a gentle jog and settled in the saddle, gaining ground without posting. The sun had blasted the last of the green from the sparse grasses and weeds, turning the world tan under an azure sky. He doubted there was feed within fifty miles. Brown's cattle would be edgy, starved, hollow in the flanks, and ready to stampede. Like Brown and his men.

An hour later he reined the bay atop the knoll he had so often used to spot the herds from Texas. Sure enough, off to the southwest a golden cloud billowed upward, the dust raised by thousands of hooves. It hung in the windless air, an eerie haze that enveloped the herd and its riders. He watched a long while as the herd made its slow way north, ever closer.

It was time. He heeled the bay down the sere slope, and headed toward the distant herd. He knew that all but the point men would be wearing bandannas over their nostrils, and those on the east flank and the drag would be suffering from the terrible dust. Brown was likely to be riding point, so that was where McCoy headed. But first he removed his suit coat and tied it down behind him. His bare white shirt and unburdened belt would send its own message to men with guns.

The closer he got to the herd, the higher the dust rose into the sky, until it seemed to reach zenith, like a terrible thundercloud blotting out the sun. A subtle rumble saturated the air, and he knew he was listening to many thousands of hooves. He had never seen such dust, not in all the years he had met Texas herds. A mile out, he could make out the point riders, and at half a mile, he discerned three men leading the herd. They saw him and rode in his direction.

He reined up. The bay twisted nervously under him, alarmed by the trembling earth, the yellow sky, and the thunder that seemed to rise from the bowels of the world.

These three rode good Texas cow ponies and pulled up before him. They had all been roasted to the color of chestnuts and slimmed down to bone and sinew.

"I'm McCoy. Welcome to Opportunity," he said. "I'm looking for Mr. Brown."

"I'm Brown," said the man in the middle, sitting up to stretch his legs in the saddle. "These here are Jack Hardesty and Dinty the Drill."

McCoy nodded and lifted his hat. Hash Brown was the one man of the three the broker would not have guessed to be the cattleman. He had a burnt round face, a receding jawline, a soft and timid look about him, and mild gray eyes. His body was as round as his face, slope-shouldered, big-bellied, thin-necked. The other point riders were both burly and short and at home in the world. One was blue-eyed, twitchy and cocky, the other silent, brown-eyed and phlegmatic.

All three carried sidearms and rifles in saddle sheaths and looked fully capable of using them. But Brown hardly seemed the man of legend and gazed at McCoy with mildness in his face.

"I'm the livestock broker in town, Mr. Brown, and looking to do some business."

"We'll get to that. Where's the best bed ground? These beeves are plumb thirsty, and they haven't seen good grass for days."

"There's none left, Mr. Brown. It's all been eaten down for fifty miles. You're the last herd."

Brown weighed that. "How far to water?"

"Little Arkansas is three or four miles ahead. It's running low now, and there's a lot of mud. You'll end up pulling a lot of beef out of the mud. If I were you, sir, I'd try to keep this herd from water for another mile or two after you reach the river. The Little Arkansas runs northwest. Keep going past Opportunity. Might be a little green grass down in the river channel and water enough."

"Obliged, Mistah McCoy. Will you ride with us and talk some business?"

McCoy nodded. Who was this amiable, round man with a receding chin?

CHAPTER 32

The little slope-shouldered Texan was an enigma. McCoy rode beside him, furtively examining the man and his point riders. They certainly seemed familiar with firearms. Each of their looped belts bristled with cartridges. Most cowboys didn't haul that much firepower around. A loaded belt like these weighed plenty.

And yet, this stubble-cheeked man seemed the soul of courtesy.

"Ah've brought two herds, you know, Mistah McCoy."

"So I've heard. About forty-five hundred?"

"That's how we started. They're over six thousand now."

McCoy processed that a moment, not daring to ask how the herds mysteriously grew. But Brown answered the silent question.

"We bought a few along the way, but mostly Ah'm acting as a consignor for an outfit that didn't make it. The C Bar. Trail boss got sick. Ah've got the papers."

"You'll need them, sir. The railroad's strict about that."

"Anyhow, Ah've got around five thousand of my own, and Ah'm consigning another thousand. We stopped to road brand the ones we picked up, so everything's in order."

"Is your other herd in the same condition as this one?"

"Ah reckon."

"So if I look these beeves over and make a price per head, it should hold for the other bunch?"

"They're just about the same. Maybe the one behind's a bit lighter, seeing as how they got even less feed."

That was fair and forthright. McCoy had to admit the cowman was dealing squarely.

"Well, sir, here's what I propose. I'd like to ride through the herd with you and get some idea of the weight and age. After that, I'll make an offer for all adult stock, no spring calves. They're a loss to me. The prices in Kansas City are better now than a month ago, when the yards were swamped with Texas cattle. They're offering twenty-three or twenty-four a head now, depending on weight and condition. In July it got down to twenty and a half.

"I buy for less and take the delivery risk, and hope to profit from the difference. I charge two dollars a head delivery, and that pays for my men, who ride with the cattle to the yards and feed or water them if necessary. If I have to ship to Chicago, I lose money on that. If I can deliver to Kansas City and St. Louis, I break even or do a bit better."

"Ah understand, sah."

"I've ordered stock cars, all I could get. I've enough here to ship stock now. I can process at the most about twelve or thirteen hundred head a day at the shipping pens, so it'll take five days to move your herds out of here. Now, about the pay? I can offer you a letter of credit, gold, cash . . ."

"Greenbacks, sah. All greenbacks."

"That's a lot of cash. Are you sure it'll be safe?"

"The world's not a safe place, but Ah have means."

"Cash, then. You're talking at least a hundred twenty thousand dollars. The bank doesn't have that kind of cash on hand. But I can wire for funds. They come overnight from KC in the express cars."

"You gonna pay me beforehand, Ah reckon." The casual question hung there.

McCoy didn't want to. "What I propose, sir, is to pay you each day, in installments, for twelve hundred beeves at a time. I'll pay for those each evening, and you deliver twelve hundred to the loading pens first thing in the morning. Always assuming we can agree on a price."

"Ah reckon that's fair enough."

McCoy approached the pricing gingerly. "Mister Brown, if these cattle are light, I may not be able to offer —"

"Ah already got that reckoned out."

"What I can do, if you're not satisfied, is —"

"You have a good reputation, Mistah McCoy. Now, as long as we're doing business, what's this Ah hear about this town of yours treating Texicans bad?"

"It's true, sir. But there's also a reform movement afoot, and I think things will change swiftly. I've told the mayor that if this continued, you Texans will take your business elsewhere next year."

"Not hardly a boy going south that didn't stop to tell us how he got gypped. They were a bit riled up."

"My guess is, Mr. Brown, that those things won't happen to your boys."

"Men, sah. Ah never call them boys."

"Men they are. It takes courage to come up that long trail, fighting weather, stampedes, rivers, snakes, and all the rest, including cold and misery sleeping on hard ground. I admire them, every one."

"You'll do, Mistah McCoy. Now how's about you and me riding through, and you can see what Ah've got here."

Addison McCoy followed the fabled Texan into the plodding herd, all the while wondering whether he had just gotten lucky, or whether all this amiability concealed something darker. Brown had business to do. He had cattle to sell and no grass to feed them. The faster he got his beeves loaded into stock cars, the more money he would make. Whatever fate he and his rough men had in mind for Opportunity, it probably would wait until the last of Brown's stock rolled east.

The moment he and Brown plunged into the herd, he found himself choking on dust, which churned upward and coated his shirt and trousers. The cattle were all gilded with it, and it lay so thick on them that he could scarcely read the signs of health and weight. But his practiced eye did, bit by bit, see what he had come to see. This herd was not in bad shape, all things considered. One more week of this and it would be. Haste was essential.

It was hard, in that whirl of golden dust, to calculate the age of these beeves. It was even hard to guess at their gender. He knew he would be making, at best, a sophisticated guess, and that he might get burned.

He prowled another half hour, until he felt so gritty he wanted only to ride up to the point, and fresh air. Brown followed him through the clumps of cattle, taking just as much grit as the broker. Then McCoy motioned, and they put their dust-shrouded horses into a fast walk, and awhile later emerged near the point.

McCoy pulled out a big bandanna and wiped the grit out of his nostrils, eyes, ears, and off his face.

"Mr. Brown, can you tell me how many are bulls, steers, cows, young stuff?"

"Ah don't believe Ah can, especially that bunch we're taking with us."

"Steers?"

"No steers. Ah've never cut a beeve."

"What about age?"

"This bunch is younger. After the War of Secession, we rounded up old critters, running wild all those years. Now, this bunch is different."

McCoy swiftly calculated and came up with twenty dollars and seventy-five cents. He really wanted to offer twenty and a half because he was buying half-blind.

"Mr. Brown, how about twenty and six bits?"

"Twenty-one. That's how Ah was figuring."

"Twenty-one if I can cull up to a hundred animals. And if we ship fast. I think these will be in trouble in less than a week."

"What do Ah do with the culls?"

"Sell them at a lower price. Sell them to local butchers. Sell them to me for eighteen, nineteen. Sell them to local stockmen for twelve or thirteen."

Brown poked out a hand. McCoy gripped it, wondering what the next days would bring.

"Ah'd like to pay my men, Mistah McCoy. Could you fetch me the greenbacks, twenty-five thousand will do, and I'll deliver to your pens at dawn?"

"All I can do is ask Garrity — he's the banker — if he has that much in the vault. If he does, I'll accommodate you."

"If he doesn't, Ah'll settle for what he's got and ship that many at dawn. The men, they've been on the road four months; five months, some of them, getting our herds lined up down there around Alice. They'll be wanting some fun."

Thin ice again. McCoy decided to plunge ahead. "Mr. Brown, I advise the men not to carry much cash. But I think they'll have a fine time anyway."

"Ah understand."

"If any get into trouble with the law, contact me. I'll do my best."

Brown nodded.

"There's a firearms ordinance, and it's enforced."

"Ah reckon the boys can leave their irons in the camp."

McCoy wondered whether he was hearing right. Was this the man that every busted and bitter Texas cowboy vowed would scorch Opportunity? Were these the Confederate veterans who would raze the town? Was this the cattleman who had broken other cattle brokers in other railroad towns, chiseling down the price, threatening mayhem?

The herd now moved within sight of Opportunity, and McCoy could see the bridge. It was mid-afternoon.

"I'll leave you here, Mr. Brown. You keep on going two or three miles northwest, and then bed your herd. There'll be water, and you might even find some grass in the riverbed, if you're willing to pull out mired cattle.

"I'll try for twenty-five thousand in currency

and return as fast as I can. I do business on a handshake. I honor my handshakes. Every Texas cattleman I've ever dealt with has honored that handshake. We'll start loading as soon as we have some daylight."

He left Brown and his point riders and headed into town, feeling awash in dust. He could scarcely see the blackness of his twill suit. He arrived at the bank fifteen minutes later and headed straight into Garrity's office.

"Brown's here. I'll need twenty-five thousand cash if you have it in the vault."

Garrity looked startled. "Let's see," he said.

A short time later, McCoy had his bank notes in a satchel; Garrity had wired Kansas City for more cash, and McCoy started out to the bedding grounds. As he crossed the tracks, he noted the presence of a pair of burly gents in gray bowlers lounging on the station platform.

He hoped they wouldn't be needed.

CHAPTER 33

Angie wandered through her plant upon light feet, almost as if she were floating. The sun's rays streamed through the grimy windows, dancing on the Hoe company's famous press and streaking the benches. She touched the warm steel of the press where the light struck it, and touched the pine case boxes and the grainy newsprint. She touched the sticky ink barrel and drew a finger across the rough-textured type lying in the bed of the press. This was her sacred place, and she was returning to it in triumph. No one stayed her. She had won.

Earlier, she had printed another hundred copies of the paper for subscribers and advertisers. Then she had gotten Stanislaus the hardware man to drop by and saw off Marty's padlock and unscrew the hasps. Now the place was hers again, unscathed, holy, an altar that could not be defiled. She felt its goodness as something almost tangible. Newspapers sometimes published sad news, or contentious editorials, but mostly papers were the beacons of their communities.

No one, not Marty, not Sid Wannamaker, not any of the policemen, disturbed her, and she knew they wouldn't. Why bother? She had exposed corruption, and now it was public knowledge and there was no story to suppress. She had endured hardship, even a stint in Spade Ball's jail, but none of that had kept her from printing several editions that bore witness to the injustices of Marty's ring. She planned to follow through with more stories and editorials, but now things were in the hands of the citizens of Opportunity. They would either clean house or accept their corrupt government.

Gideon had always seen such things as abstract ideals. He had a vision of good civic order in America and applied that yardstick to what he saw in the city. Her approach was more maternal. Opportunity needed mothering, guiding, rebuking, and encouraging, all with tenderness and love.

She wandered about, relishing the sense of possession that engulfed her. But then she began work. The first task was to bill advertisers, collect for the last ads, and sell the next ones. She would meanwhile break down the issue that lay in the chases on the trucks, until it was only a memory. And then she would collect news and begin the whole process once again for the issue due six days hence.

In a euphoric mood, she measured the ads, wrote invoices, and addressed the exchange papers. Then Aunt Gladys Busby walked in.

"I saw the door open, so I walked in, expecting to find that beast in here. I was going to thwack him with my parasol," she said.

"That beast is my son," Angie replied. "But I'm glad you're here. We've work to do."

"They put you in jail."

"For a little while. It was educational."

"It was criminal."

Gladys parked her parasol, glared around her, and sniffed.

"It's dirty," she said.

"A newspaper is always inky."

"Men are dirty, not newspapers."

Angie laughed. "Would you do the ledgers please? I'm going to go sell ads and try to collect some overdue accounts."

"I wish they'd come put me in durance vile. I'd tell them a thing or two. I'd wear out Spade Ball just telling him how evil he is. Then I'd wear out his deputies. Then I'd wear out the justice of the peace."

"It's over, Gladys."

"You think so; I don't. Never think that men are up to anything good."

"Do you include your late husband in that indictment?"

Gladys sniffed.

"We're here, you and I, and we're running a paper again. I want you to carry on, just as before. The past is dead. This lovely town will clean itself now. I've new concerns.

"We've a dangerous Texas cattleman in town, and we must alert our readers to be wary of his cowboys and stay in at night. We're going to do some articles about the cattle shipping business and maybe get some improvements. We're going to talk about a new mayor, a new judge, a new police force. We're going to endorse good people.

"I haven't even started in on the school system. If we don't do better, we'll have children who can't even read this paper. There isn't a doctor in town except that old drunk. And only one dentist. And no infirmary. And no poor farm. We're going to promote good things here. I'll do stories, and I'll want you to write editorials because you're good at it."

"I just wish Spade Ball would arrest me and drag me right down Kansas Street howling like a coyote, past hundreds of people, and put me in jail," Gladys said. "I wouldn't be as temperate as you about it."

"I'm going to the post office with the exchanges, Gladys. Maybe if you're lucky you can be arrested."

Gladys lifted her jaw slightly and turned her lips downward. "I will be ready," she said.

Angie smiled, plucked up the addressed papers, and headed toward the post office. In a way, this final act, sending out the exchanges, would seal the fate of the administration. The eyes of Kansas would be upon Opportunity. It seemed almost like a sacramental act, this last exposure of misconduct to the sunlight of public opinion.

She discovered a dozen people in Horatio Bates's bailiwick, all clamoring for their mail, which had just been posted. The postmaster was busily plucking letters out of pigeonholes and snatching parcels from a table.

A woman she knew slightly turned and stared at her.

"You're Mrs. Drum," she said.

Angie nodded.

"You may cancel my subscription. What kind of mother would belittle her own son in public?"

People stared.

Angie chose not to reply, but Horatio Bates did, from behind his counter.

"A courageous woman, that's who. A woman who loves her son so much she wants to rescue him from perdition."

The woman was not mollified. "If I were Mayor Drum's mother, I would be supporting him."

The issue seemed to divide the crowd a moment, and then it passed. People collected their mail and vanished.

"Well, Angie, you're mailing out the big issue?"

"I had to print some more early this morning. Fifteen exchanges again."

Bates nodded, totted up the postage, and began applying stamps while Angie dug in her pockets for cash.

"What next, Angie?"

"It's over. I won. I'll just keep on trying to make Opportunity a better place to live."

Bates stared. "Are you so sure it's over?"

"Horatio, once a secret is out, it's out. All that

effort was simply to keep me from saying in public what Marty's ring was doing. They can't put the cat back in the bag."

"I'm not so sure."

"Well, I am. Marty's going to face opposition. Magnus Garrity's weighing in. Marty'll resign, along with the whole police force and Sid Wannamaker, or else they'll get pushed out."

Bates shook his head. "We'll see. But I'll say this, Angie. You're a woman of great courage."

"Oh, Horatio," she said, and hurried out.

On Kansas Street, the wind carried the sound of bellowing cattle to her ears, and she knew that Addison McCoy was shipping once again. She detoured south, passing Lone Star Street, and another block to the Santa Fe rails where the pens stood. A hubbub rose from the pens, and hundreds of bawling cattle swirled around in them. Cowboys, colorful in chaps and wide-brimmed hats and bandannas, were sorting them out and driving them up a chute and into stock cars.

She thought she saw McCoy standing next to the chute, but the dust obscured all the men. And beside him was a round and unprepossessing Texan, holding a tally board. She guessed that must be the dreaded Hash Brown, but she saw no evidence of trouble. The cowboys were working. Some railroad detectives watched quietly. No one was upset or angry. Business as usual. And business as usual was just what Opportunity needed just then.

272

The town had been spared trouble.

She looked around, wanting to see Marty, or Spade Ball, or any of Spade's deputies, and saw no one. That made her uneasy. One or another of the police were always on hand to keep an eye on things. Maybe Spade had the good sense to keep his head low and avoid trouble. Surely that was it. Marty had probably laid down the law to the marshal: don't bother this dangerous crowd. Let them ship their cattle, enjoy a night or two in the saloons, and go home.

She walked slowly back to the paper, uneasy. A town needed the protection of its lawmen. Even corrupt lawmen. But there were none in sight. Impulsively, she hiked up Kansas to the jailhouse and peered in. No one was there, and the cell door was open.

CHAPTER 34

Angie turned to leave the empty office only to discover Spade Ball at the door, glaring at her.

"You!" he growled. "What do you want?"

His appearance shocked her. The normally natty marshal had a stubbled face and great black bags under his eyes, begrimed clothing, and mud-fouled boots.

"I'm beginning a story about Hash Brown and his big shipment," she said. "It must be the largest in our history. But no one was here. Is anyone keeping the peace?"

He glared at her as he headed for his desk. He was wearing a brace of revolvers. "I suppose *The Outlook*'s going to stir up the animals."

"No, Spade, I'm quite concerned about this city's safety."

He glared. "Well, maybe you've discovered we're worth something after all. You can quit worrying. What do you take us for? I've deputized ten men. We're at the bridge night and day, and bunkered in, too. No one comes into Opportunity armed. I've got twelve men on duty plus me. I work them in shifts. Three are forted up at the bridge behind barriers, and one's patrolling the town."

"That's good, Spade."

"You're damned right it's good. Those Hash Brown boys haven't caused a bit of trouble. Last night, they came into Lone Star Street, had a few drinks, lost a little at cards or dice, and rode out. Nicest little bunch of angels I ever saw."

"All those threats," she said. "Do you think it was all talk?"

"No, it wasn't all talk. But they can't do much without their shooting irons. If the lid blows, we're ready. We'll toss the whole lot into jail. We've got McCoy's railroad detectives, too, at least until the loading's over and the beef's on its way to cow heaven."

Spade unbuckled his heavy holster belt and laid his blued steel artillery on his desk. She saw weariness in him. People had told her that Ball was the best lawman in the West, able to handle dangerous characters, disarm fools, get out of tight corners. She wished his ethics were as good as his other skills.

"Well, if you're treating those cowboys well, they'll treat us well," she said. She scarcely expected the detonation that followed.

He sprung out of his chair. "What do you know about it? Do you think firing words is the same as firing bullets?"

"No, Spade —"

"I'll tell you something. Texans are like kegs of gunpowder. They're different from other men. You never know about a Texan. They're ten times prouder, ten times meaner, ten times more thin-skinned than anyone else. They get into fistfights and brawls just to beat on each other. Just to prove they can fight.

"I'm tired of Texans. I don't know whatsa matter with them. Maybe that sun fries their brains. Maybe their daddies never licked 'em when they was running wild. They take offense at anything I say. If I ask them, real soft like, to cool off, they get madder. They're like them longhorns. Like a bunch of bulls goring each other, and when they get tired of that, they go pick on anyone they can find, especially sheriffs and marshals."

"Maybe they're just worn out from months on the Chisholm Trail. Is that so bad, blowing off some steam?"

"Blowing off steam ain't the same as treeing the town."

She smiled, remembering the bookish one who had visited with her at the beginning of the shipping season. "Not all are wild," she said. "Some are gentlemen."

"All are animals," he snarled. "You've got your news. Go tell the town that we've got things under control. Marty and I've put a lot of thought into it."

"I will. You treat those boys kindly, and they'll return the favor."

"I'm tired of your opinions," he snapped.

She nodded. The colloquy had come to an abrupt end.

She stepped into the sunlight, a story forming in her mind. She had to give Spade Ball credit, and maybe Marty, too. They had acted to preserve the public safety. She might as well talk to Marty about it. He'd growl, and then boast about safety. And she would have an upbeat story.

She headed south, crossed sleepy Lone Star Street, quiet in the morning light, and walked into Marty's emporium. The big hall seemed deader than ever, though she knew it was an illusion. Evenings, it seemed to radiate light and energy. She waited a moment for her eyes to adjust, peered about, and saw only emptiness. She didn't even spot a bartender. So she retreated, rounded the corner, and climbed those thunderous wooden stairs up to his rooms. At the landing, she knocked.

"Yes?" from within.

"It's me."

"What do you want?"

"I'm doing a story."

"I'm sick of your stories."

"About public safety. About doing a good job keeping the peace here."

Silence. Then the door opened. Marty glared at her, and she could see he was as exhausted as Ball, unshaven, in rumpled clothing, owl-eyed. Keeping a lid on Hash Brown's men had taken a toll. He nodded her in.

"What's happening, Marty?"

"What's happening? I try to run this town

good, and all I get is my teeth kicked in by my own mother."

"It's *well,* Marty, not *good.* I try to run this town well . . ."

Suddenly he was laughing and shaking his head. "That's all I need, a grammar lesson."

Angie grinned.

"You won," he said. "I told Spade to lay off Brown's outfit. Just let 'em drink themselves out of cash and get out of town. Nothing's gonna happen unless they get into brawling and fighting, and so far, they're behaving like choirboys. They ain't choirboys and Spade'll throw them in the jug and cool their heels if they mess around. We're gonna enforce the ordinances here. They haven't got a sixgun between them, and we've got more marshal badges pinned to more shirts than we ever had around here. So it'll be all right. You satisfied?"

"It's *isn't,* not *ain't,* Marty."

"Beat it! You wrecked the town finances, and now you're wrecking me." But he was laughing.

She smiled, stood, and left. She had a story. She had run her corruption stories. Marty would probably be forced out of office. But she hadn't lost Marty.

She trudged up Lone Star Street feeling euphoric. She had slain all the dragons.

When she arrived at the paper, she found everything in good order. Aunt Gladys, who exerted more force than the dowager empress of China, had completed the ledger, accepted two

letters to the editor from men supporting reform, sold four classifieds, one card, refused
one display ad for patent medicines that were
loaded with opium, and written an obituary
supplied by Jasper Dill. A youth, William Gatz,
had died of consumption after a year-long
struggle. Angie had known the boy; briefly he
had been one of her carriers, but was too weak-
ened by the disease to continue. Sadness stole
through her. Willie had never stopped trying.

"Gladys, I got a good story this morning.
There's been no trouble and probably won't be."

"Oh, Spade Ball's going to find a way to start
some."

"Gladys, that's cynical."

"It's a godly observation upon the nature of
the male sex. I don't know why the good Lord
made the sexes."

Angie did, but held her peace.

She decided not to write the story just yet.
This was the second day of shipping, and by its
end, a third of Hash Brown's longhorns would be
off to Kansas City. Maybe his cowboys would become more and more rowdy and trouble might
start. Maybe Brown himself would start something. But a story was certainly brewing, and the
next issue would feature it on the front page.

She turned to other things: breaking down old
ads, setting classified ads, looking at exchange
papers for news she might use, ordering newsprint and ink, and studying prices for a new
font; this one was wearing out.

Only a few days earlier she had been torn to pieces, her love for her only son at war with her love of justice and honor. Only a few days earlier she had sickened, fevered, wearied of life because her soul, mind, and body could no longer survive divided and torn.

Her *Outlook* had sprung to life from its ashes like a phoenix. She had stuck to her principles, and her principles had won, or would soon if Magnus Garrity's reform group succeeded. The town government would be better off without Marty, but Marty was not without means. He was bitter, but the relationship had not ruptured. Even Spade Ball was behaving — for the moment — and she felt secure because of his diligence.

She had no time to celebrate all this; the paper lacked a compositor, and the entire burden of typesetting and press work fell upon her. But need she ask for anything more?

Gideon would have been proud of her, and she yearned to share all this with him. She had lived up to his high standards, stuck to her guns, and weathered indignity, abuse, and even jail. Soon she would walk up the river road and then up a gentle grade to a bluff overlooking the Little Arkansas and find his gravesite. Some day she would lie beside him, a single stone marking the place. But that was far away.

As soon as she could, she would sit down in the tawny grass of August and talk to him.

"Gideon," she would say. "I stood up for what was right, and it all turned out well."

CHAPTER 35

Addison McCoy was not a man to borrow trouble, but in some moments he thought things were going all too well. Where was the thunder that Hash Brown carried on his shoulders?

Each evening, twenty-five thousand dollars in small-denomination greenbacks arrived in the Santa Fe express cars. Each evening, under armed guard, he paid Brown the cash, and early the next morning, his men delivered another twelve hundred longhorns to the loading pens.

The Kansas City stockyards were paying a good price, given the light weight of these beeves, and McCoy was making a modest profit. Wisely, McCoy had refrained from exercising his culling option until he could see the second herd, and then he culled animals he didn't want. The second herd came in hungrier and lighter, and McCoy knew he would do little more than break even on the final twelve hundred.

The Santa Fe was cooperating, returning stock cars swiftly, and supplying him with every railroad dick the company could spare. Some of these gents stood out; beefy types with lumpy suits and a certain wary look about them. They were experienced men, used to dealing with hobos, rebellious gandy dancers, train robbers, express car safecrackers, pickpockets and swindlers in the passenger trains, punks who stole timber and iron and wire and spikes; and the occasional lunatic passenger who caused a scene. Cowboys they could deal with. One of the railroad's agents was a woman, Amanda, who passed herself off as a gambling lady of the demimonde, and circulated in the saloons. She was, he learned, capable of squeezing secrets out of randy cowboys, and did not scruple in the means she employed.

Spade Ball was cooperating, too, especially with his checkpoint at the bridge. No sidearms slipped into Opportunity over that bridge, but McCoy sometimes wondered how many were arriving by other means. A guarded bridge could scarcely prevent determined men from transporting all the weapons they chose. The nearest ford of the Little Arkansas was ten miles upstream. Heaven knew where the nearest rowboat might be concealed.

Apparently Drum's Ring had decided not to fleece this crowd of cowboys, and as far as McCoy knew, Brown's men drank and gambled and whored on Lone Star Street to their hearts' content, unmolested by the law. That was another phenomenon. Here were two score of trail-weary cowboys, as thirsty and rowdy as any bunch up the Chisholm, and yet they contented themselves with sipping drinks, flirting with barmaids, losing small amounts of their meager pay at keno, faro, roulette, poker, or monte, and hiking now and then into the poorly lit shacks of the girls of the line.

Where were the brawls, the knifings, the rattle of gunshots, the wild drunks, the boasting and daring, the rowdy horseplay, the broken glass, and shattered chandeliers? Plainly, some ruthless hand was restraining them. With what? A promise of blood sport later?

That's why McCoy worried. But a man could worry about a lot of things, and there wasn't much point in it.

Sometimes he thought that Hash Brown was simply a smart businessman: make money, get cash, avoid trouble. The man had been a confederate officer, and it showed. His whole outfit displayed military discipline. Somewhere out on the bedding grounds, a small fortune in greenbacks was being guarded by tough men. There were never more than twenty of Brown's cowboys on Lone Star Street, and these stayed oddly subdued. What's more, they all left town at midnight, riding out together. By day, a dozen or so were working in the shipping pens while the rest stayed out on the bedding grounds.

McCoy made an effort to get to know Brown, but was usually rebuffed. And Brown always turned aside, in that polite Southern way of his, any tenders of friendship or even conversation.

"Ah'm not much for talking, Mistah McCoy," Brown said after McCoy's second attempt. "We'll just do handshake business, straight and true, and let it go at that."

"I've always wanted to talk with you about the war. We faced each other, you know. I didn't know that until I began reading after it was over."

"The war's a closed subject, sir."

The way Brown said it led McCoy to believe it was not a closed subject at all, but a running sore.

"Well, would you join me for lunch? We've business to attend."

"The railroad station's good enough for any business."

And so they did their business in the cramped ticket office, surrounded by the telegrapher, stationmaster, and clerk, and under the watchful eye of the chief of the Santa Fe's detectives, Carlos Brook. Sometimes Brown stored his daily payment in the small stationmaster's safe until he could take it out to the bedding ground. Unlike other cattlemen up from Texas, Brown did not rent a hotel room and ended each day by riding across the bridge and into the vast and empty prairies.

McCoy had exercised his hundred culls by the end of the third day, but then helped Brown sell the culled beeves to a Kansas rancher, Josiah Crisp, for twelve dollars a piece cash. That money, too, vanished into the bedding grounds.

On the penultimate day, McCoy found Carlos Brook lounging around the station and drew him aside.

"Almost over, Carlos. There's one thousand twenty-three to ship tomorrow, and that's it. I'll pay Brown tonight when the westbound comes in. We should have the rest of those beeves loaded by early afternoon tomorrow.

"I don't know what's going to happen then. But I want you and your men to stick around an extra day or two. If anything's going to happen, that's when it will come — after Brown's collected his cash and disposed of every beeve he owns."

"Can't do it, Addison. We work for the railroad, not the town. We protect railroad property. Not a one of us has a badge."

"Well, could you at least delay shipping out? Stay tomorrow night? On the ground that the station needs guarding?"

Brook shook his head. "I don't see a thing wrong. Brown's another businessman. He ain't gonna get himself in very serious trouble; ain't gonna get the federal army or Pinkerton's or anyone like that on his back. He's a cattleman now. Why make trouble? What's in it for him? Life as a fugitive if he tears up the town? Nah. That stuff, it was all gossip and threats and nonsense. We spend a lot of Santa Fe cash tracking down legends that all come to nothing."

McCoy didn't agree.

He hiked over to the jailhouse and found Spade Ball there, munching a mashed potato and gravy, blue plate special from The Wagon Café across the street. The man looked worn.

"Spade, we're finishing up tomorrow, midday. The railroad's running a special with the last of Brown's cattle on board. If anything's going to happen, it'll be tomorrow."

Ball looked annoyed. "You think we don't know that?"

McCoy ignored the testiness. "I don't think your bridge barricade's going to keep sidearms out if Brown's got plans for this town."

Ball glared.

"You've done a good job at the bridge," McCoy said, "town's not suffered a thing."

Ball's hostility didn't dissolve, so McCoy headed over to the bank, his last stop, and caught Magnus Garrity there.

"Magnus, if anything's going to happen, it'll be tomorrow. That's when Brown has his cash and his beeves are riding the rails. Given all the threats we heard, I wouldn't put it past him to invade this bank."

"We've a good safe, Addison."

"Brown commanded some sappers during the war."

Garrity smiled. "Let us handle it," he said.

The bank president sounded as though he had made some plans, but whatever they were, he was not confiding them to McCoy, not even after many years of working closely.

"All right, Magnus. I just wanted to let you know."

Magnus smiled, clapped a hand on McCoy's shoulder, and steered him out of the office.

McCoy thought maybe to alert Mayor Drum, but decided against it. He had not seen Marty Drum the entire period, but knew from the gossip that Drum was staying close to his rooms and his saloon. Any of those evenings, you could find Drum sitting quietly in a corner, watching Brown's cowboys. He wasn't hiding, exactly, but Marty Drum wasn't wandering around town, either.

McCoy waited for the five-ten westbound to pull in, and when it did he took receipt of the final twenty-five thousand from the express agent and carted it under the guard of the railroad dicks, to the stationmaster's safe while Brown and one or two of his top men watched. This final payout would be a little different. Not until the beeves were tallied in the railroad pens the next morning could McCoy and Brown do the figuring and come up with the final settlement.

He stuffed the satchel into the Santa Fe safe, knowing that Carlos Brook and his men would guard it well.

"All right, Mister Brown, there it is. You bring in the beeves as usual, we'll tally, and you'll have your cash before any board the stock cars."

"Ah appreciate your diligence."

"I've enjoyed doing business with you. I hope you'll come next year and choose me as your livestock broker."

Brown smiled, but said nothing.

"Board," yelled the conductor. He waited a

moment, and then plucked up the steel step stool and climbed into the vestibule of the first coach.

They watched the four-four type Baldwin passenger engine with its big drive wheels spit steam from its pistons, hiss, chuff sooty smoke from its diamond stack, and slowly ease forward. The couplers rattled taut, and the Santa Fe westbound, the express car and three coaches, abandoned Opportunity.

Brown and his men clambered aboard their cow ponies and rode across the bridge.

Later at the brass rail in the Stockmen's Hotel that evening, McCoy heard that not one of Hash Brown's men was enjoying the nightlife on Lone Star Street that night.

CHAPTER 36

There in the stationmaster's office, Addison McCoy counted out twenty-one thousand, four hundred ninety-two dollars, all in greenbacks. Hash Brown watched, and when McCoy had finished, Brown counted the same stacks while McCoy watched.

Out in the pens, Brown's men were harrahing the final shipment of longhorns into the slat-sided cattle cars. This batch looked lighter than the previous ones, and McCoy doubted that he would break even, much less make a profit. But he didn't mind. The other shipments would turn a good margin.

Three lumpy railroad detectives looked on; two of Brown's men chewed on toothpicks. Just outside, on the wooden platform, Spade Ball lounged against a post pretending he was invisible. McCoy felt sweat leak down his armpits and soak his shirt, though the air was mild this early in the morning and the window sashes had been shoved as high as they would go. The still air carried the sounds of bawling cattle, whistles, yells, and the crack of whips, but the only sound from within the room was the soft exhalation of air.

McCoy stuffed the remaining three thousand five hundred eight dollars into its canvas bank bag, which he placed back into the Santa Fe safe. He would pick it up later. Brown's hands slowly peeled bills, counting them out and placing them back into neat stacks.

At last he looked up.

"Ah thank you, Mistah McCoy. Trust that everything's satisfactory?"

"It is, sir, and I trust the same is true for you?"

"Well, yes, you've been impeccable, sah."

"Then I hope to see you next year."

"No, Ah don't reckon you will."

"You'll be shipping somewhere else?"

"Yes, somewhere else. Maybe Newton. That's a coming place, Ah hear."

"But not Opportunity."

"There's a deal of sentiment about your town, down where Ah come from. Lotta men riled up some about the treatment here. Lotta talk. But Ah suppose you heard plenty of it."

McCoy sighed. "There's reform underway here, Mr. Brown. Plenty of citizens don't like injustice of any sort, and I think you'll find things better for your men next year. If not —" he shrugged. "Maybe I'll see you in Newton, or Dodge City, which is doing a fine business, too."

Patiently, the sun-stained Texan bundled his bills into a black canvas satchel. Then he buckled the bag and slowly stood. Years of hard work had bent him, so that he was hinged forward at the waist.

"I guess that does it, Mistah McCoy."

"You have plans? Would you join me for lunch?"

Brown shook his head. "We'll finish loading and watch our beeves go down the rails. It's mighty kind of the Santa Fe to run an Extra, so they don't suffah more." He pulled a turnip watch from his jeans. "Looks like we'll be pulling up stakes around eleven. Then we'll just ride."

That was it. Brown and his men headed toward the pens, where their horses stood at a hitchrail, and McCoy watched him stuff the black satchel into a large, behind-the-cantle saddlebag, and strap it down thoroughly.

Carlos Brook dug dirt from under his fingernails with a jackknife, then folded and pocketed it.

"We'll be off this afternoon, McCoy. We're done here."

"Wish you'd wait."

"Anything happens now ain't the railroad's business. I got three going on the three-fifty westbound, and the rest of us will catch the five o'clock to KC."

"Well, thanks for your help. I'll see you off later."

Brook shrugged.

McCoy collected his satchel, found Spade Ball outside, and motioned toward the bank.

Ball walked beside him, nimble and quick, up Fourth Street and across Lone Star Street toward Kansas Street.

"How'd all that go?" the lawman asked.

"Too well," McCoy replied.

"Maybe that's it. Brown's a businessman, pure and simple."

McCoy thought of all the threats he'd heard, all of them coming to the same thing: Hash Brown would do the honors for Texas.

"Could be, but I wouldn't count on it."

"I'm not. We're guarding the bridge tonight and tomorrow, and I'm keeping my special deputies under oath."

They reached the bank, and McCoy arranged for his cash to go into the vault. The young teller Willie Nation counted it once again and issued a receipt. Ball watched idly, and then meandered away.

McCoy stood in the sun, hoping a breeze would dry his sweat-soaked shirt. The whole town seemed serene, quietly baking in the August sun. The soft sound of mooing cattle drifted his way, and he knew he must return and see to the loading and also that two of his hands, Joe and Mike Sandstrom, were in the caboose.

Brown's men were loading the last of the longhorns when McCoy returned. The pens stood empty, dotted with manure that smelled sharply in the heat. It had become, actually, a pleasant smell to McCoy, one that any cowman knew meant business.

The Santa Fe had a Mogul engine coupled and steaming. The Sandstroms waved at McCoy from the caboose. McCoy watched the stationmaster walk out, hand a slip of paper to the engineer, who nodded. Then, with a wail of the whistle and the huff of steam from the pistons, the Extra jolted to life and slowly churned eastward. Brown and his men watched from the other side of the pens, and then mounted their cow ponies and rode south toward the bridge.

McCoy noticed that Ball stood at the bridge, watching them pass by. Then Brown's men reached the far side and dwindled into specks upon the rolling plains.

It was not yet eleven.

McCoy didn't stop sweating, and that irritated him.

He noticed Ball walking toward him and waited for the marshal.

"McCoy, this afternoon let's you and me make sure they're out of here. I'll meet you at two at the livery, and we'll ride out to that knob where you glass the country looking for herds. We'll look together."

"All right."

"I'm sending two men out along the river, too, one each way. They're to ride five or six miles and keep an eye out for anything."

"Good idea."

Spade Ball was a fine lawman, no matter that he had sticky fingers. McCoy climbed wearily to his office upstairs in the station and collapsed into a chair, not understanding why he felt exhausted so early in the day. Desultorily he updated his ledger, still sweating even though a good summer's breeze whipped through the windows.

He heard noise on the stairs and discovered Angie at the door.

"Brown's gone?"

"Far as we know. We loaded the last of the beeves and sent them to KC an hour ago."

"No threats?"

McCoy sighed. "Yes, in a way. He said he's not coming here next year, and he doesn't think any outfit will."

"Mind if I do a story?"

"Be my guest."

Angie wasn't one to waste a minute. While she scribbled on her pad, he described the last big shipment of the year, spoke at length about Brown, who had surprised him with his Southern courtesy, and then focused on what interested Angie the most: the casual way that Brown had said that Opportunity's cattle shipping business was over.

"That's big news," she told McCoy.

He nodded. "May not be true, though. Especially if" — he was always embarrassed to call it Drum's Ring — "the town gets cleaned up."

She nodded. "What Mister Brown said, that's the best thing that could happen, Addison. I'll play that at the top."

He agreed.

"Do you think we're in danger?"

"I don't know. This afternoon, Ball and I will have a look south of town."

"When you get back, let me know."

"Sure, Angie."

At two, he hiked to de Vere's livery and found Ball there, saddled up, and his own bay saddled as well.

"You got your glass?" Ball asked.

McCoy checked his saddlebag and nodded.

They passed the checkpoint at the bridge and boomed across it in a fine, dry breeze. At last McCoy's sweating had stopped. They rode across caked clay land, stripped of grass in every direction. Already summer storms were cutting ditches in country that had been denuded of its vegetation for the past six years.

"You figure Hash Brown's up to something?" Ball asked.

"Yes."

"Me, I think he's a smart businessman. Them Texas boys are all brag and boast, but Brown's smarter."

McCoy shrugged. That was the last of the talk until they steered their mounts up the gentle knoll and stood atop it, their gaze encompassing a vast country scorched by the sun. Not a cloud plowed a shadow across the land. Not a telltale puff of dust caught the sun.

McCoy pulled out his brass field glass and studied the whole area, seeing nothing. The marshal did the same.

"You got the experienced eye, McCoy. You see anything?"

"Nothing."

"Neither do I. Brown's gone to Texas."

"Don't count on it."

Ball smiled. "I'm not. I'll keep a man at the bridge all night."

That seemed a small comfort.

CHAPTER 37

The whirlwind gathered and blew into Opportunity, the freshets of air lifting leaves and bending grass. The whirlwind spun around the town, out of the lonely prairies, out of the moonless night. The whirlwind burst into Opportunity, patrolling the streets. The whirlwind rattled doors and shivered windows, eddied air into homes and stores. The whirlwind swept through the alleys, touching everything, wavering the flame in the few lamps still lit, including the ones in *The Outlook*.

The whirlwind burst into the stationmaster's office and caught the night telegrapher unawares. Traffic was light, and he was dozing. The eleven-thirty eastbound freight had left. Nothing would arrive until seven-fifteen in the morning. The whirlwind poked a double-barreled shotgun at him, and he raised his hands. A man with a soft Texas voice sat down in his seat.

The whirlwind caught the temporary deputy at the bridge, surprising him from behind and carrying him away. A Texas man assumed the deputy's place behind a small barricade. The whirlwind blew into Marty Drum's Lone Star

Saloon, extinguishing the coal oil lamps and frightening the half dozen customers, the sole remaining card mechanic and the sole barkeep on duty. The whirlwind raced up the stairs to Mayor Drum's flat, flattened his door, and caught him in bed, wearing nothing against the sharp breeze. The whirlwind prodded him to the city jail and penned him there in his cotton nightshirt and twill britches.

The whirlwind yanked the covers from Spade Ball's bed, tugged him out of it, paused while he dressed, and then swept him down to the jail and penned him there. The whirlwind collected his deputies one by one, Eddie Farrar first, and then the temporaries, and tugged their weapons out of their grasp.

The whirlwind burst through the rear door of the handsome shiplapped home of Justice of the Peace Sid Wannamaker, catching him in his white nightshirt, terrorizing his wife. The whirlwind paused to let him dress, let him gulp water to slow his pounding heart, and then harried him to the city jail. The howling wind drowned out his petulant protests.

The wind howled into the homes of Jasper Dill, Ed Wilber, and Joe Pflug, surprising them in their safe and secure sleep. The wind carried double-barreled twelve-gauge shotguns upon it, the black bores pointing here and there and everywhere.

The wind chased alderman Mo Baskin into his back yard and dragged him out of his outhouse, and the wind caught Arnie Marlowe saddling a horse in his carriage barn, and the whirlwind whipped all these, too, into the crowded jail. Some men wept.

The whirlwind cornered city clerk Dinky Smothers in his closet, and yanked him out of it. The wind tackled Billy de Vere who was ascending the ladder into his hayloft, yanked him down, and hustled him to the jail. The wind burst the door of the fine turreted home of Magnus Garrity, banker, and blew chill into his soul. The wind marched him to the jail in his yellow silk bathrobe and slippers after he resisted, and tossed him in with the others.

The whirlwind posted well-armed men on the roads out of town, on the riverfront and other key places, such as Billy de Vere's livery barn, where horses and saddles and escape might tempt people, and before the dark stone bulk of the bank, and before Ed Wilber's darkened Mercantile, where one might find firearms and ammunition.

The men newly caught in the jail said little. Beyond those thick iron straps, half a dozen Texas men eyed them meanly and waited for something. While they were waiting they unloaded the city marshal's racked weapons, one by one, and pocketed the ammunition. Each Texas cowboy carried a large-bore scattergun as well as his sidearms, and between them they could control a large crowd.

The burghers of Opportunity gaped at one another, sleep-shocked, terrified, sickened. Some glared at Spade Ball, who hunkered in a corner, or at his deputies, who slouched against a cold stone wall. All of them feared for their lives and wondered how many minutes more they would live.

There had scarcely been a disturbance, and not one shot had been fired. Nothing louder than a surrendering door, shattering glass, and a few yells had troubled Opportunity that midnight, though someone with a good ear might have heard weeping.

Marty Drum did not like the way his own people were staring at him and turned his back to them. He knew what they were thinking. They were ungrateful. Maybe they were remembering that his administration had built this fine, escape-proof jail, which they all saw as the city's cash cow. Unlike the others, he felt certain he would survive this night. If Hash Brown meant to kill, he would have completed the butchery an hour earlier.

The overcrowded pen began to stink as men sweated fear and dread out of their pores. But nothing happened, and Drum began to think maybe the Texans would lock them there for the night, hurrah the town, and leave after a whooping ride down Kansas Street.

He was wrong. Another of the Texans entered.

"Court is in session," he said. "We'll start with Drum, Wannamaker, Ball, and Garrity.

You four come to the door. The rest stand back."

Marty, Sid, Spade, and Magnus clustered at the door. The rest huddled against the rear wall, terrorized by the shotguns lowered at them.

The Texans freed the first four and marched them across Kansas Street to the city hall, also Marty's creation, and the justice court, which Marty had thoughtfully planted next to the city clerk's office so that people could pay their fines right into the town's coffers.

The prisoners were ushered into Wannamaker's courtroom, which was well lit with half a dozen coal oil lamps throwing a sickly yellow light over the assemblage. There, behind the bench, stood Hash Brown, and what an astonishing sight he was. Marty blinked, not recognizing the man at first. This Hash Brown was cleanly shaven, well scrubbed, and wore a black cutaway, a boiled shirt, and a floppy black bow tie. He looked like a lecturer at some college, or maybe a supreme court justice.

"Come before the bar, gentlemen, if that is the propah way to address you. As you see, Ah'm wearing ceremonial costume that is fitting for the grave events that will transpire here. Nothing less will do. Clothing speaks its own language. One sees such attire on morticians, judges, and sometimes preachers."

Now, at last, Marty Drum felt the icy breath of death blowing upon him.

Brown's soft Southern diction commingled

with something else; something taut, shrill, and intense.

"Come forward, Ah say. Come up close now and receive your *justice*."

The prisoners did. Marty stared into eyes brimming with sulphur and brimstone, eyes that radiated hellfire.

"Ah, that's better. Now Ah know what's going through your minds. You think we're looking for revenge, that Hash Brown's the Avenging Angel, just as you've been told by plenty of Texas men you've impoverished. Ah'm not.

"Justice, entirely and absolutely *justice*. Ah'm going to restore every last cent to those you've euchred, and not one more. This court will operate exactly along the lines of the Honorable Wannamaker's court, which is to say, no trial, no jury, guilty as charged without exception, and if anyone protests, that's a fine excuse to raise the ante. Any objections? Is that not perfect *justice?*"

Sid Wannamaker shrank into himself.

"Will any of you call it vengeance?"

No one spoke.

"Now, in some ways, you'll get off lightly. Ah wonder how many Texas men suffered how many days in your jail yonder. How many had headaches from all those gun barrels landing on their skulls. You'll escape headaches and jail because we're not planning to visit your fair city long."

Marty felt the beginnings of hope, but that

deceptively benign light in Hash Brown's eyes worried him.

"Now, Mistah Garrity, since everything depends on you, Ah'll begin with you. We're not without our informants. We know you're interested in reform, and we've nothing personal against you. But you're the custodian of a lot of money ripped from innocent men. We're inviting you to open your safe for the sake of *justice*."

"I could not do that, sir."

"Bravely spoken, Mistah Garrity. A banker's courage. But in this case, we're not requiring you to disgorge any funds except those of the miscreants. Every other account will be safe. You can choose not to, if you wish, and no personal harm will befall you. But if you so choose, sah, Opportunity will soon be ashes. Your stone bank building will stand alone in a field of coals. So what will you gain?"

Garrity swallowed and said nothing.

"Ah'll let our banker ponder that while we proceed. City Marshall Ball and Justice Wannamaker, come to the bench. . . . Ah, that's just fine. Now, what would you recommend that your sentence be? This court's more lenient than yours, Mistah Wannamaker. Ah'm consulting with you. Would you say that we could fashion justice out of injustice? Ah, you're silent. Maybe that's wise. Silence conceals whatever lies in the souls of men.

"Well, let's just see now. One of you plucked

innocent Texas men off of your streets, the other found them guilty and fined them all they possessed, and if they protested, fined them all the more. The details don't matter. Some Texas men forfeited bail. Others received kangaroo justice. Most of them were shaken down in the jailhouse, deprived of the last dime hidden in their boots. Is that not so?"

He paused. "Well, fashion me an appropriate punishment!"

Ball glared. Wannamaker sulked.

"All right, Ah'll do it myself. Everything you possess is confiscated. Your funds in the bank, your property. You sent Texas men into the wilds, broke, without means, without weapons, and they had some bad times getting back home. That's how it'll be. You'll receive a horse and clothes on your back, and you'll *git* and never return. You and your deputies. This pleasant little town of Opportunity will never see your faces again and be all the better for it. Your ill-gotten funds will be returned to those you stole them from."

Ball stared rigidly.

"And now you, Mistah Mayor. Now you," Brown said.

CHAPTER 38

Wearily, Angie wiped down the press. A stack of tomorrow's papers was drying. In the morning she would fold them and give them to her newsboys.

It was a good issue, concerned with public safety, reform, and the final burst of shipping. Aunt Gladys had penned a fiery editorial about the need for reform, but Angie had toned it down. Civility lay at the heart of leadership. If she wanted Opportunity to heal, then finger-waggling was something to avoid.

It had been an odd night, punctuated by the clank of her press. In the quiet moments she had heard through her open windows occasional shouts and disturbances, but nothing more than usual when Texas cowboys were in town.

Then, just as she was plucking up her shawl to walk home, the double doors parted and she beheld two cowboys, no doubt Hash Brown's men. But these two carried shotguns.

"We're closed," she said.

"You Angie Drum?"

"I said I'm closed."

"You come with us, ma'am."

She paused a moment. These two weren't behaving like rowdy cowboys. She had better find out about this.

"Are you asking me, or abducting me?"

"We're taking you to the justice court, Mrs. Drum."

"I choose not to go. You are trespassing. You are not the law. This is private property, and you will leave at once."

"Sorry, ma'am. You're coming, even if we have to drag you."

"It's called kidnapping, and it is a criminal offense, I believe."

For an answer, the shorter one grabbed her elbow and began steering her out the door.

She resisted. "Where's Spade Ball? I insist on seeing him."

"Either in the jail or the court, Mrs. Drum."

"Who's requiring my presence? Sid Wannamaker?"

They didn't reply. She felt herself being pushed bodily into the street and finally surrendered. Walking beat being dragged.

The night seemed peculiar. An armed man was standing in the doorway of Ed Wilber's Mercantile. Other armed men patrolled the streets, all of them carrying shotguns. *The Texans had taken over the town.* Fear welled up in her. She was on her way to a meeting with Hash Brown.

They escorted her through the door into the small courtroom, and there she discovered Hash Brown behind the bench, amazingly attired, and Marty and others before him.

"Ah, there you are, Mrs. Drum," Brown said. "Ah trust you had a pleasant walk. We're performing small acts of *justice*. Ah wanted you to see them. We've just stripped your judge and your marshal of everything they possess, and shortly, we'll send them packing with the clothing on their back and nothing else. Their stolen wealth will be returned to its rightful owners.

"All of Texas honors you, ma'am. You had the courage to speak up, print truth, talk to us in our sorrows. A brave woman, setting aside a mother's love for the love of righteousness and *justice*. Ah thought you might enjoy what's transpiring here. We're just about to mete out justice to your boy, the Honorable Martin Drum."

"Stop this at once," she said. "This is a kangaroo court, not justice."

Brown rapped the butt of his revolver on the bench and glared at her, then Marty.

"Mistah Drum, Ah'm inviting you to fashion your penalty. That's more than Sid Wannamaker did for the men of Texas."

Marty kept quiet. Angie thought he looked desperate.

"You're leaving it to me, then. Well, let's see, Mistah Drum. There's all the money in city accounts that shouldn't be there because it was stolen by your ring. There's all that cash in your safe, money you were going to use to buy out your mother to shut her up."

That startled Angie. How did this Texas cattleman know so much?

"But there's other matters to settle up, Mayor Drum. A good Texas man named Bo Waggoner killed himself and the reasons lead straight back to the Lone Star Saloon. Ah understand Mistah Waggoner was winning fine and handsome at faro until you rung in a crooked dealer, and then you stole it all back. Now, it's true he should've quit, but your ladies had been plying the man with spirits to befuddle him, and before he knew it, you'd cleaned him out of an entire year's income, leaving starving sons and unpaid drovers. What do you say, Mistah Mayor Drum. A life for a life?"

Marty shrunk into himself.

Angie froze, a turbulence coursing her veins. Hash Brown eyed them all lazily, taking his time. Ball and Wannamaker and Garrity were aghast.

"Ah guess maybe I'll let you off lightly, Mistah Mayor Drum. You just open that safe in the Lone Star, hand over every cent of it to my men, and we'll give most of it to the Waggoner boys, and maybe dish the rest out to their hands, if we can find 'em."

"I won't open that safe! That's my life savings in there."

Brown sighed. "Guess we'll open it ourselves. Ah've a pair of sappers from the Army of Texas ready. And one more word of protest and your saloon will be hot ashes."

Marty wilted. He would submit.

"Speaking of opening safes, Mistah Garrity, have you come to your rightful decision?"

Garrity nodded, dourly. "I will open the bank safe," he said. "And I will report you to authorities tomorrow, you blackguard."

Brown smiled. "It does beat burning down a lot of homes and businesses belonging to good folks, yes it does."

Angie stared at this ghastly man and his ghastly court.

"All right, take these gents out. Joseph, you and Will take Mistah Drum to his safe and don't forget the jug of coal oil to pour over the floor if he changes his mind. Drew and Scat, you take Mistah Garrity to the bank and collect what's owing to the men of Texas. And Billy, you just take the judge and marshal back to jail for the time being."

They were waiting for the next round of prisoners, and Angie saw a chance to rebuke the man.

"Mr. Brown, this isn't a court, this isn't justice, and you have absolutely no right to do this. Stop it at once and leave this town."

He stared at her. "You stay quiet, little lady. Ah'll do what's required for justice."

"Justice! Who are you, God? You're a private person, not even a citizen of Kansas! This isn't justice, it's your revenge."

"Hush your mouth, Angie Drum. You're making me think you're part of Drum's Ring after all."

"I'm on the side of what's right, not your side, and not the side of the mayor's ring. And this drumhead justice isn't right. Two wrongs don't make a right!"

Brown rapped softly on the bench with the butt of his big revolver, tapping patiently, his raps matching her words, fires dancing in his eyes.

Some of his men brought in the next bunch of prisoners, including the city councilmen, city clerk, and a few merchants who'd backed the ring.

"Order here, order. You gents just step forward and hear your sentence. Like your fine outstanding judge, Mistah Wannamaker, I've already decided you're guilty. My little task is to impose *justice,* an eye for an eye. Now then, Drum's Ring. That's next. Mo Baskin, Arnie Marlowe, Dink Smothers. Like fatted calves ready for the slaughter."

He laughed, while the prisoners blanched.

"You even *look* fat," Brown said. "You want to impose your own sentences? You have the chance. That's more than Sid Wannamaker offered Texas men. Go right ahead. Tell me what you think's fitting, what your groveling and repentant souls are whispering."

No one spoke.

"Ah thought so. Ah'll do it for you. Herewith, your bank accounts and such valuables, like gold, as we can transport, are confiscated in the name of justice, and all such funds will go south with us to Texas in the name of justice."

He laughed softly while the city officials glowered.

"Come hither, Billy de Vere. You were part of the ring, and many a cowboy lost his horse because he couldn't pay a feed bill because your ring emptied their pockets. How many good Texas saddlers did you commandeer and sell, Billy?"

"They owed me," de Vere retorted.

"Well, you owe Texas. Herewith, your bank account's confiscated, your livestock's confiscated, your wagons and anything else of value's confiscated."

Angie felt outrage boiling through her.

"You're worse than the ring," she snapped. "At least they kept order. Your men fanned through this town, breaking into homes, trespassing, dragging people from their beds, terrifying women and children, abducting people like me. Did you have a warrant? Did you have the slightest legal or ethical right to do any of this? Are you the law? What sort of justice is this?"

"You . . . hush . . . up, ma'am."

"I won't. I'll speak my mind. This may be the frontier, but we have courts and law, and you're free to go to any Kansas court and get your due. You're no judge, no jury, and no prosecutor. You're nothing but a vigilante mob."

"Ah'm warning you, Miz Drum, Ah'm warning you for the last and final and irrevocable time. If you won't listen, it'll go hard on you."

But she would not.

"Justice! Is that what you call this? It's simple banditry, mean as you can make it. You call it justice, but it's rage and darkness and dishonor. I'll fight with my paper for the true justice due every Texas drover who came up the trail. But this isn't justice."

She heard the tapping of the gun butt on the counter, the tapping that matched her words, louder and louder.

"The war's over," she said. "We live in a civil society. Law rules us. There are proper ways to redress wrongs, even on the frontier. My newspaper is one. Come tell your story, and I'll print it. The district courts. The governor. The attorney general. Do it the right way, and you'll have real justice. Stop playing God, deciding the fate of others with a wave of your hand."

She saw the heat in his eyes, and wildness, but she couldn't stop.

"Go back to Texas where you belong," she snapped. "You aren't civilized enough to be here."

The tapping stopped. The courtroom stank of sweat and coal oil smoke. She heard not a breath. Hash Brown's face had stained red beneath that sun-stained flesh, red with heat and rage. Then, slowly, without a tremble, he turned the revolver around and gripped its butt, his finger finding the trigger.

She saw the black muzzle of his revolver, she saw the hammer cock, and she heard the crack, and felt herself driven away, away.

CHAPTER 39

Horatio Bates knew nothing of all these terrible things until the next morning. He had slumbered peacefully through the momentous night. Even when the bright sun coaxed his eyes open, tugging him from the arms of Morpheus, he knew nothing. Not until well after he had arrived at his post office, unlocked, and opened shop for the day, did the awful news reach his ears.

There, upon a tide of tears, did he learn that the one he treasured most had been murdered, and that Opportunity had forever changed. Later, he could not even remember who had told him. There had been a clamor of shrill voices.

So shocked was he that he shuttered his post office contrary to regulations and drifted to the green enameled bench in front of city hall and sat dumbly, unable to fathom this new universe.

But out of the many voices he had learnt the story. Angie had simply goaded Hash Brown into firing. For her, vigilante justice was just as evil as the ring's graft, and she had not been afraid to say so, even to the judge and jury and hangman. Those present had gaped as Angie slid to the floor, a bullet hole in her forehead, dead even before she fell.

Among those who gaped at Angie was Hash Brown himself, who quietly set the deadly revolver on the bench and stood. They said she lay on the floor with her eyes wide open, and that even in death there was sight in them, strange, magical sight. They said Brown had peered down on her and shrank back, rebuked by that terrible gaze.

"Ah didn't mean to do that," he had said, and those words had flown through Opportunity on wings of fire.

Brown had stood there fully a minute, and then sprang to life.

"This changes things," Brown had said. For a minute he paced, and then issued new instructions to his Texas cohorts with a curious staccato bark rattling from a strangulated throat. They say he never again touched the murder weapon, the black Peacemaker that lay on the bar of justice, a thing so evil that it lay there still, orphaned by its own darkness. Brown walked away from that courtroom, no longer judge and jury, but the butcher of justice.

Within the hour, Brown's outfit had fled Opportunity, but not before taking unusual precautions. Word of the murder reached the bank after Garrity had opened the safe, and Brown's men had examined the accounts of everyone in Drum's Ring and removed the appropriate sums from the shelves. Swiftly, Brown's men abandoned the process, leaving the shaken Garrity alone to lock up. Word reached the Lone Star Saloon just after a surly Marty Drum had opened his safe and Brown's men had emptied it. They had left him sprawled in a chair, weeping.

By the time Brown's men left town at two in the morning, they had ripped out the two telegraph keys and thrown them into the river, cut the telegraph wire, released everyone from the jail except the marshal and his deputies, and kept the keys; driven all of the horses in Billy de Vere's livery barn before them as they crossed the bridge; and then poured coal oil over that timbered structure and ignited it. The bridge had burned for two hours, throwing a ghastly liverish light over the town before collapsing into the river. They had made a clean getaway and would probably make the Nations before anyone in Kansas could form a posse and give chase.

That morning, town people had fished one of the telegraph keys from the river, repaired the line, and notified the world. Mayor Drum had locked himself in his rooms and was refusing to see anyone. Jasper Dill had taken Angie away. In the absence of any leadership, people begged Magnus Garrity to restore order. Garrity summoned a grieving Addison McCoy, and they became the de facto government.

They put the hardware men and blacksmith Joe Pflug to work sawing the iron straps of the jail, and had ordered food and drink for its inmates, who sat sullenly within, soaked in silence. They had shot telegrams to law officers within a hundred mile radius. And they had posted handwritten notices around town that there would be a town meeting that afternoon.

McCoy found the postmaster staring into space.

"Horatio, I've appointed myself to look after Angie's funeral," he said. "Marty's locked in his room, and what we hear is that he's drunk and incoherent, and not in shape to do anything. I want you to do an eulogy. You knew her best, admired her most."

"I could never do her justice, Addison."

"None of us can. But you will do her more justice than the rest of us combined."

"I couldn't stand up there —"

"Of course you can. Two o'clock tomorrow. Dill says that this heat . . . there's no time. He's making a coffin."

"And worrying about being paid, I imagine."

"I told him I'd pay if Marty can't manage."

Bates snorted.

"You come to the town meeting, Horatio."

"What's going to happen?"

"We're going to quiet this town if we can. Magnus and I went up to Drum's rooms and forced our way in. We talked him into resigning. We've the signed letter. Wannamaker skipped out. He took the westbound an hour ago. Mo Baskin and Arnie Marlowe promised to get out

316

by tonight under threat of indictment. We'll prosecute Ball and his deputies if we can, if they don't flee the coop. We've made Billy de Vere the town marshal for the time being. We'll report all this, and also what was taken from the bank. The city's funds are gone, along with everything in the accounts of Drum's men. Many of the town's saddle horses are on the other side of the river, but we expect to get them back. The news, apart from Angie, isn't all bad. We'll also talk about a special election and a reform ticket."

"I'll be there," Bates mumbled.

McCoy patted him affectionately on the shoulder and left the postmaster to his grieving.

Bates rose and walked slowly along Kansas Street in the bleak sun, wanting to remember Angie in her lair. He found the paper unlocked, just as she had left it when Brown's men had abducted her in the middle of the night. He stepped through the double doors and into a hushed quiet. No one was present, not even Gladys Busby. Sun streamed in. He had the feeling he had entered a church, and maybe that sense was not amiss. In a small, humble, secular way, a good newspaper performed the rites and offered the comforts of a church. And sometimes bad papers did the work of the devil.

He wandered through the plant, seeing her two printing smocks hanging on hooks, her slippers under her desk, an umbrella on the hat rack. He drifted into the printing shop and found the edition she had printed the night before dried and stacked neatly, ready for the folding and delivering. He picked up a copy and read it slowly.

Her last edition was very like all the others, literate, well wrought, well printed, and wise. He read her story about the final shipment of cattle for the season, and another about concerns for public safety in town. He read Gladys's tart editorial insisting on reform. How the lady did thunder. Angie didn't rail; her views were always understated, almost apologetic, but all the more forceful for that.

This was Angie's last paper, seeking the betterment of life in Opportunity, pouring blessings out upon each person in the town. Angie had set the standards, voiced the ideals, raised the sights of everyone who read her papers.

Angie . . .

He gingerly settled into her desk chair and let his memories of her sharpen in the awful quietness. They wanted him to speak at the funeral, and he didn't know what to say. He yearned for that burden to be taken from him. Marty should do the eulogy. Marty was her son.

But that line of reasoning ended swiftly. Marty knew her least of all.

Bates tarried there, missing Angie, until he heard the eleven o'clock westbound pulling out, its mournful whistle echoing through town. That meant the mail had come. Bates had a duty and lumbered to his feet to do it. The mail would be delivered.

He found resentful people awaiting their mail and soon was sorting out the day's post. Life went on. With the posts came news of loved ones, answers to anxious questions, payments and bills, notices of death and birth, thank-yous, penny postcards from faraway places. All these he hastily pigeonholed and then handed to the quiet people.

He found a curious comfort in his work, for if delivering the mail reminded him of anything at all, it was that life went on. Few of those who wandered in that day even knew Angie, and not all of them approved of her. He didn't doubt that there were some who thought she had got what was due her.

The work did not take his mind from Angie. In fact, he worked by rote, scarcely attending to his business because the things Angie had done and written occupied him. Little by little, as memories freshened, he was gathering the strands of what he would say at her farewell.

When at last he had the incoming mail sorted and the outbound mail stamped, canceled, and loaded, he realized he had missed the town meeting that Magnus Garrity and Addison McCoy had gathered together on Kansas Street in front of the city hall. He doubted that he had missed much. And what he had missed he soon would hear because it was the fate of postmasters to hear all things.

But little news reached him that day, and he locked up that evening in the midst of melancholia. Instead of going home, he drifted back to *The Outlook*, and there found Gladys Busby sitting in her usual place, her cheeks wet.

"Oh, Horatio, we've lost her," she cried, and folded into his arms.

He drew her tight. "We've lost her, Gladys," he mumbled. "But she left us an inheritance."

CHAPTER 40

Horatio Bates dressed himself as best he could for a man careless about clothing, and now he stood before the looking glass, dissatisfied. Angie would be disappointed to have her eulogy recited by a man with a gravy stain on the sleeve of his black gabardine suit coat and small cracks in his newly blacked shoes.

But he could not help that, not on such short notice. He walked along Kansas Street until he had reached Third and then headed a half block north to Jasper Dill's Mortuary and Furniture Store. A small crowd had settled onto Dill's wooden benches.

Jasper Dill, arrayed in a black cutaway, motioned him forward and gestured him to a reserved seat. Before Horatio, on draped sawhorses, lay a burnished oaken casket, plainly an expensive one, and atop it rested a bouquet of marigolds and hollyhocks.

Horatio peered about, looking for Marty, and discovered him at the rear of the hall, cheerfully greeting people as they arrived, that odd cocky grin on his face. An unseemly smile, Horatio thought. Gladys Busby occupied a nearby seat, a soft conical presence in slate gray silk, her gaze imperious and censorious. He saw none of the city police attending, nor any of Drum's Ring. But some of Opportunity's businessmen were dutifully on hand, probably more with an eye to avoiding criticism than to grieve.

Angie had no particular church affiliation, and McCoy had rounded up a Presbyterian, Stephen Watts, to officiate. Promptly at two, the mourners were invited to rise and sing "Rock of Ages," and then Mr. Watts, who didn't know Angie well, discoursed on life and death and the purposes to which we are born, and the reasons mortals suffer.

Then, suddenly, the reverend was beckoning, and Horatio found himself walking to the lectern. He quieted his taut body, looked over this forlorn handful, and began.

"We are gathered to celebrate the life of one of the most magnificent women ever born to the American republic," he began. "Angie Drum's burning wish, which governed her every act, was to improve the human condition. Each issue of her newspaper issued forth with that underlying message to the world. This America can be a better place if we wish to make it so.

"She always regarded newspapers as special, maybe even sacred institutions, whose single power, the ability to throw light upon darkness, publicize goodness as well as evil, gave them unique power . . . and unique responsibility. This responsibility she had perfected along with her husband, Gideon. Every issue of *The Out-*

look had sought to make this place better, kinder, more charitable . . . and more just."

He sensed that his congregation wanted to go home, so he hurried along.

"There are those who think she was merely partisan, siding with the Texans against the citizens of this town. And in the end, there were Texans who discovered she was not siding with them, but with the American vision of good civil order, with properly constituted courts of law, and government that rules with the consent of the governed.

"Those who think she was a partisan are mistaken. Her allegiance belonged to the virtues, not to parties or factions, or gangs or administrations. She was on the side of justice, mercy, honesty, kindness, and civility. Whoever violated these basic decencies discovered in the pages of *The Outlook* that lamp of exposure that is the dread of those who would rather do their deeds in darkness.

"So deep was this commitment that Angie Drum let nothing, not family ties, not even fear of boycotts, cancellations of subscriptions, and threats upon her person, sway her from her duty. And thus she laid before us the need of reform, and thus she laid before us the accounts of gross injustices, pocket-lining officials and lawmen, innocent sojourners in our midst stripped of every cent and thrown onto the prairie with nothing but their clothing.

"Did it matter to her who performed these

deeds? Deeply. Yet she saw the need for reform and resolutely fought for it. In the course of those struggles, attempts were made to silence her, reduce her advertising, buy her out, persuade her to cast her gaze elsewhere. But she never wavered. When her own plant was padlocked, she found a way in and produced a paper that threw more light upon the darkness."

Horatio knew he was making this body of mourners uncomfortable, and yet he had to say a few more things. He paused, letting all that sink home. People were glancing at Marty, but Horatio didn't much care. Let Marty suffer behind that plastered grin.

"How many citizens of Opportunity supported her? Very few. Why? Because of how their bread was buttered. They paid no property taxes, and this city's government funded itself to some degree with the sordid fruits of injustice, the shakedown of innocent people. And so this evil was countenanced widely, and consciences were numbed, and the upright citizens of Opportunity averted their eyes and pretended not to notice the robbery in their midst.

"We honor the best of Americans. This country was founded in hope, in the belief that here, with a new land, we could fashion a better system than whatever existed in the old, tired nations we all emigrated from. Let us now honor Angela Drum, mother and saint and patron of Opportunity.

"Like the soldiers who surrender their lives

for our country and its liberties, so was Angie a soldier who surrendered her life for the commonwealth of our souls. We honor the fallen."

He sat down in the midst of quietness.

The cortege made its way north, up the gentle grade to the Opportunity cemetery, and they buried Angie next to Gideon with a simple prayer amongst those marigolds and hollyhocks.

EPILOGUE

Six years later I stopped at Opportunity. I was on my way to Washington City to consult with the post office about a new posting.

The town had shrunk to a village of fifty, sleeping somnolently in the autumnal breezes, perhaps living on its memories. One would never have imagined just from looking around that it was once a flourishing, blustery cowtown of two or three thousand. Few of the buildings even remained, and what had happened to them was a mystery to me.

The Texans never came back after that year. They took their herds to Newton, or Dodge, or other places until there were no more drives and the railroads took over. I stayed on only a few months. When it became plain to the United States Post Office that a full-time postmaster was no longer needed, they contracted the postal service to Ed Wilber, who handled the mail from a corner of his store.

Opportunity never became the county seat. Hutchinson won that one, largely because of the corruption that the legislature discovered in Opportunity. And after that, the town simply leaked away like sand pouring through cracks in the hourglass.

Marty Drum stayed on, behaving oddly, all things considered. Within a week of Angie's murder, Marty reopened his saloon, his usual cocky smile pasted across his face, his bonhomie loud and inappropriate. It was as if he had never cared about Angie at all, and I, for one, think that the man had no feelings about his mother, and even less sensitivity to those ideals and values Angie tried to instill in him.

I don't know what happened to Marty. One day, about when I was being transferred, he shut down the Lone Star, boarded a train, and I never heard another word about him. Angie would have been disappointed that her final sacrifice did nothing at all to transform her boy.

For years I followed the Hash Brown case. The State of Kansas tried repeatedly to extradite him for murder, but three Texas governors refused to honor the extradition, and Brown was never brought to Kansas for trial. So great was his grip upon southern Texas that no politician dared to bring him to heel. Neither have I ever been able to find out whether Hash Brown actually returned that cash he took with him to Texas, money he had claimed would repay all those cowboys, money that would go to Bo Waggoner's sons.

But I did, finally, discover a small news item one day. A coral snake had bitten Hash Brown in the neck during a roundup, and he had died within an hour.

When I stepped off the Santa Fe train, I swiftly discovered that Opportunity had become only a whistle stop. I told the agent I would be departing on the next eastbound, at six-thirty, and he promised he would flag down the train.

I hiked the mile to the graveyard and found the marker. DRUM it read. GIDEON AND ANGELA. They had chiseled in Angela's date of death in 1877. I took off my hat and wept for an American heroine.